READING LEVINAS/ READING TALMUD

READING LEVINAS/ READING TALMUD

An Introduction

IRA F. STONE

THE JEWISH PUBLICATION SOCIETY
Philadelphia • Jerusalem
1998 • 5758

Manufactured in TK
Library of Congress Cataloguing-in-Publication Data

   Stone, Ira F., 1949–
      Reading Levinas/reading Talmud : an introduction to the philosophy
   and method of reading Talmud of Emanuel Levinas : with readings of
   selected talmudic passages using his method / by Ira F. Stone.
         p.   cm.
      Includes bibliographical references and index.
      ISBN 0-8276-0606-0
      1. Talmud—Criticism, interpretation, etc. 2. Levinas, Emmanuel—
   Contributions in interpreting the Talmud.   I. Talmud. English.
   Selections.   II. Title.
   BM504.2.S76   1998
   296. 1'2—dc21   97-38779
                                                                  CIP

Designed and Typeset by Book Design Studio II

02 01 00 99 98 97
10 9 8 7 6 5 4 3 2 1

For Annie

Publication of this volume was made possible by gifts from:

Mark and Judith Benjamin
Richard Bailey and Patricia Marcus
Peter and Esther Damm
Edward and Leanna Meinstein
Joel and Marcia Migdal
Peter and Gail Shapiro

CONTENTS

3

PREFACE

This book constitutes an invitation on my part. With it, I invite you into two worlds that I have inhabited simultaneously over the past decade and more. That it is a personal invitation accounts, in large part, for the point of view of the book. That is, *I* am writing it for *you* and have tried not to hide behind any authorial screen. The pronoun "I" is used often. This is not usually the way "scholarly" books are written. However, despite what I believe is a healthy dose of scholarship necessary for the writing of this book, it is not a book of scholarship. Its goal is not to prove this or that scholarly point. Its goal is to entice you into my world.

My world is neither the world of Emmanuel Levinas nor the world of the Talmud. My world is the intellectual and spiritual environment in which I live because I have encountered both Levinas and Talmud and, following Levinas's lead, because I have attempted to bring those two worlds into discourse *within me.* This book is both the result of that interior discourse and an invitation for you to attempt to do the same.

In order to help you enter the world of Emmanuel Levinas, I have tried to present to you his thought as that thought resonated in my soul. In order to help you enter the world of the Talmud, I have read selected passages from the Talmud according to principles that I derived on the basis of my reading of Levinas. The purpose of both parts of my book is not to present an authoritative reading of Levinas or of Talmud, but to invite you to read both and produce your own book, whether in actuality or within your soul.

Underpinning the connection between Levinas and Talmud, and justifying the profitable reading of each in the light of the other, are Levinas's project for escaping the totality of the Western philosophical tradition and his recognition of the Talmud as a vehicle for exhibiting a literary discourse in which this escape is, in fact, accomplished. Therefore, I would like to emphasize this point even at this preliminary juncture and make sure that this essential idea—totality—is understood, in order for it to be overturned.

Traditional philosophy can be said to be holistic. That is, it is a mode of thought that identifies the self with reason and extends itself outward through rational analysis to include everything it encounters. *To understand* everything is to make it rationally present and, therefore, part of the same system that is doing the analysis. Nothing can stand outside this system.

From this mode of thinking we develop ways of speaking and living in the world that deny the possibility of "something" that is not the same as ourselves. Since we deny the possibility of "something" that is not the same as ourselves, everything is "ours." We can do with it as we please. This is the totalism that Levinas is responding to and the totalistic thinking that he contends lays the foundation for totalitarianism.

Levinas identifies the Talmud as an example of rational discourse, of language, that resists totality. Its logic is not that of the traditional West; its arguments do not always end in single, final solutions. It allows for the interruption of its own totality, primarily by the claims of human beings—human beings who are seen not as extensions of some impersonal self-in-being, but, rather, as approaching from outside any system I could devise to define them.

I do not want to do the work of this book in the preface. However, I think it is important to understand how I understand this connection between the work of Emmanuel Levinas and the Talmud in order to have a better picture of my world, into which I am inviting you.

ACKNOWLEDGMENTS

All of the selections from the Talmud were translated by the author on the basis of consultation with the Soncino Press edition, as well as the Mesorah Publications editions. These are wonderful resources, and I gratefully acknowledge their usefulness. Biblical quotations are from the *Tanakh: The New Jewish Publication Society Translation According to the Traditional Hebrew Text*, 1988. All of the quotations from the works of Emmanuel Levinas are taken from the translations noted in the Selected Bibliography. The section entitled "The Search for Meaning and the Meaning of the Search" first appeared in the journal *Kerem*, Winter 1992–93.

My first encounter with the work of Emmanuel Levinas occurred under the influence of my great friend Lane Gerber. His conversation and correspondence helped me more than he could know. Through Lane I came to know David Harrington, whose ability to read and critique the Levinas portions of this book helped give me much-needed confidence. Aryeh Cohen did the same for the Talmud sections of the book and was a great morning-coffee companion to boot. Neil Gillman trusted me enough to allow me to teach some of my ideas in his department at the Jewish Theological Seminary and has been a nonstop supporter. I am grateful to you all.

David Kraemer and Robert Gibbs read earlier drafts of the manuscript and were of considerable assistance. I thank you. My good friend Phyllis Laver awaited each "installment" of my work with encouraging enthusiasm. I am grateful.

My students in the Second Year Seminar of the Rabbinical School of the Jewish Theological Seminary during the academic year 1992–93 volunteered to read one chapter each from the Talmud section of this book and to offer suggestions. I am indebted to their comments for having clarified numerous points.

Each of the Talmud readings in this book originated in and through classes taught at Temple Beth Zion–Beth Israel. Our Tuesday afternoon

Talmud class helped shape my thinking in regard to most of the *sugyot* analyzed below. In a few cases the pieces were prepared for other congregational events: *siyyum baḥurim* (fast of the first-born) and *tikkun leil Shavuot* (all-night Shavuot study sessions), for example. I thank the members of these classes for their forbearance and their contributions to the all-important dialogue of Talmud study. I am grateful to the larger congregational community for its support of my learning and teaching.

Once again, my secretary, Phyllis Kramer, despite the general load of congregational work that she carries, managed to be of invaluable assistance in the preparation of this manuscript. I am very grateful to her.

Equally indispensable in checking sources and helping to prepare the final draft of this manuscript was my son Yehoshua. I am pleased that we were able to work together on this project, and I am grateful to him for giving up a few of his precious summer hours.

Dr. Ellen Frankel of the Jewish Publication Society is a superlative editor. She helped me turn this manuscript into something I believe we can both be proud of. I have learned much from her. My friend Rabbi Michael Monson, Executive Director of the Jewish Publication Society, has always been encouraging and supportive. It is especially wonderful to have a friend in such a position, and I have appreciated it, I hope without abusing our friendship.

I am again grateful to my wonderful family, Annie, Tamar, Yehoshua, and Shaul, for forgiving me a myriad of sins as I lived in the cloud-enshrouded twin peaks of Talmud *and* contemporary philosophy. I love you all.

In all these relationships and through all their love I experience the trace of Israel's God, and I am humbled. I gratefully give thanks and praise God's ineffable name.

Ira F. Stone

READING LEVINAS/ READING TALMUD

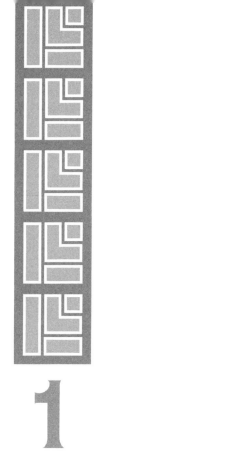

1

THEORY—
A LEVINASIAN
DICTIONARY

GENERAL REMARKS

Perhaps the most appropriate first meeting with Emmanuel Levinas should be at the dedications of his two most important books, *Totality and Infinity* and *Otherwise Than Being or Beyond Essence*. The former is dedicated to Franz Rosenzweig, the latter "to the memory of those who were closest among the six million assassinated by the National Socialists, and of the millions on millions of all confessions and all nations, victims of the same hatred of the other man, the same anti-semitism."

The philosophical work of both men was transformed by their collision with life—more specifically, with war. Emmanuel Levinas began to consider the central questions that would characterize the books mentioned above while a prisoner of war—a French soldier, a Jew, captured by the Nazi Army during the Second World War. His book *Existence and Existents,* in which he first raised these questions, was the product of this incarceration. Similarly, Franz Rosenzweig wrote *The Star of Redemption* while serving in the German army, on the Balkan front, during the First World War. For both Levinas and Rosenzweig war is the victory of totality. The totality of war helped Rosenzweig recognize that war itself was but the externalization of the totality of thought in which all of Western philosophy culminated in the idealism of Hegel. According to Rosenzweig, the totalitarianism of the twentieth century resulted when Being was reduced to Thought, and Being was falsely equated with the All. Rosenzweig would not live to see his theories borne out in the Holocaust. His warning that, through our experience, we affirm the reality of a relationship between Being and the World, between the World and Man, and between Man and Being, that such a reality cannot be reduced to thought but is in fact beyond thought and the categories of thought, beyond Being itself, and that such reality is what we call God—these prescient insights went unheeded. But these insights are what Rosenzweig contributed to Levinas: the conclusion that ontological philosophy was inadequate as a worldview to live by.

Added to his philosophical conclusions were the concrete personal losses of his parents, brothers, in-laws, and all those "closest" to Levinas. Together, life and thought, profoundly shaped in the shadow of the Holocaust, contributed to what Susan Handelman has called the "prophetic appeal" of Levinas's work (*FOR*, p. 180). We must begin our consideration of Levinas's work already burdened by his insistence that philosophy is secondary to responsibility. When we encounter Levinas, we stand already accused: Are we prepared to accept responsibility or will we reason ourselves around the impending death of our neighbor?

This is the problem of trying to introduce you to Emmanuel Levinas. Before he will allow me to disclose systematically the profoundly exacting nature of his critique of Western thought, he pushes me to implicate myself and you in the consequences of our sweet reasonableness. He forces me continually to interrupt myself because he demonstrates how all discourse that does not interrupt itself oppresses the other. But I have gotten ahead of myself. First I must answer the question: Who is Emmanuel Levinas?

Born on January 12, 1906, in Kovno, Lithuania, Emmanuel Levinas was the son of mildly prosperous parents. The family lived in the midst of the great flowering of traditional Jewish scholarship, specifically talmudic scholarship, for which Lithuania was famous. In the Lithuanian Jewish atmosphere, talmudic scholarship flourished alongside a kabbalistic tradition that combined to produce, in the years just prior to Levinas's birth, the most radical ethical pietism in Jewish history: the Musar movement, an intensely spiritual movement that represented an intellectual and behavioral alternative to the populist Hasidism that had swept most of Eastern European Jewry in the eighteenth and nineteenth centuries. Hasidism, however, did not appeal to large segments of the more intellectually rigorous Lithuanian Jewish community. At the opposite pole from this popular mysticism was the Haskalah, the Enlightenment, exposing the Jews of Lithuania to the influences of modern European life and thought. Because Levinas's father owned a bookshop, learning, both Jewish and secular, was an important part of Levinas's early experience. From the age of six he studied Hebrew and Bible.

In 1916, during Levinas's tenth year, his family, along with the entire Jewish community, was expelled from Kovno. The family settled in

Kharkov where, at eleven, Levinas was admitted as one of only five Jewish children permitted in the public gymnasium (secondary school) of Kharkov. There he read the great authors of Russian literature, the earliest stimulants to his philosophic thinking: Dostoyevsky, Lermontov, Gogol, and Tolstoy, among others.

Levinas's high-school career coincided precisely with the period of the Russian Revolution and the subsequent outbreak of ferocious anti-semitism in the Ukraine. Between 1919 and 1920, more than one hundred thousand Jews were murdered. In 1920, the Levinas family returned to Kovno, but three years later, when he was seventeen, Levinas left for France, with his family's blessing, to obtain a university education. First, he studied at the University of Strasbourg. Then, in 1928–29, he studied at Freibourg with Edmund Husserl and Martin Heidegger. In 1930, when he was twenty-four, Levinas's thesis, *The Theory of Intuition in Husserl's Phenomenology*, was published and served to introduce phenomenology to the French intellectual world. It was Levinas's book that inspired Jean-Paul Sartre to take up the study of Husserl. Indeed, Levinas was fond of remarking that Sartre had guaranteed him a place in the history of philosophy simply because Sartre credited him for this early influence.

At the conclusion of the Second World War, Levinas returned to Paris and was appointed director of the Oriental Israelite Normal School, where he remained as director until 1961. From 1947 until 1951, Levinas studied Talmud intensively under Mordechai Chouchani, who to this day remains an enigmatic and influential factor in Levinas's talmudic work. Surprisingly little is known about him. Usually referring to him only as "my teacher," Levinas attributes to Chouchani some of the basic principles of his own talmudic methodology. He intimates that Chouchani's methodology, passed from teacher to student, represents an (if not *the*) authentic method of Talmud study, lost in the chaotic destruction of the pre-Holocaust Jewish world. Mr. Chouchani's mysterious presence is also attested to in the writing of Elie Wiesel, who studied with Mr. Chouchani at the same time in Paris. Wiesel first recorded something of that experience in the chapter "The Wandering Jew" in *Legends of Our Time*. He has now added more information about his encounters with Chouchani in his memoir *All the Rivers Run to the Sea*.

However, Wiesel's accounts of Mr. Chouchani only deepen the mystery. Who was this man? Who were his teachers? Was he a link between the worlds of Talmud study before the War and after? Is Levinas's method for studying Talmud a refinement of or a departure from

Chouchani's methods? In our studies below, we will take Levinas at his word that many guiding principles of his method, which I have adopted as axioms in my own method, derive originally from Mr. Chouchani and through him to some unrecoverable past. We will, of course, review these principles in detail when we turn specifically to Emmanuel Levinas's approach to the Talmud.

The import of Emmanuel Levinas's thought is just now being felt in American-Jewish intellectual circles. Certainly among the most exciting aspects of Levinas's thinking is his bringing to bear on the Talmud his unique philosophical approach. The publication of *Nine Talmudic Readings* (Indiana University Press, 1990), translated by Annette Aronowicz, and of *Beyond the Verse*, translated by Gary D. Mole (Indiana University Press, 1994) and *In the Time of Nations*, translated by Michael B. Smith (Indiana University Press, 1994), acquaints students and teachers of Talmud with Levinas's challenging attempt to bring the study of Talmud into the world of contemporary discourse.

I propose to introduce in the first section of this book Levinas's general and Jewish philosophy, albeit briefly, identifying some of his major themes and relating those themes specifically to his talmudic hermeneutic.

THE GENERAL PHILOSOPHY

If we recognize that Levinas's philosophy is grounded in his opposition to totalitarianism and its philosophic partner, totality, we discover that what we thought was beyond the comprehension of the average person, a daunting program of philosophy, is actually comprehensible. Levinas begins his work with an insight drawn from Plato's *Republic:* that there is a "Good beyond Being," that is, that ethical behavior has as its source something outside or beyond the limits of the world whose existence we can logically account for in philosophy. However, unlike Plato, Levinas deliberately cultivates complexity in his own language to escape the confinement inherent in the language of philosophy itself, which, for Levinas, is that of ontology, epistemology, science. In this abstract language the reality of Plato's Good beyond Being is inexpressible, ineffable. Therefore, Levinas wants to find a new language not only to express the inexpressible, but to express it in a philosophically compelling fashion. To accomplish this ambitious goal, he *invents* his own language, one that is complex, filled with newly coined words and redefinitions of familiar words. Further, his style—repetitive, dense, nearly poetic, what Jacques Derrida has described as "the action of waves against the shore" (Jacques Derrida, "Violence," p. 312, n. 3, quoted in *FOR*, p. 180)—contributes to our difficulty, both real and perceived, in deciphering his ideas.

Thus, we are entangled in Levinas's own paradox: to introduce his new way of thinking into Western philosophy is difficult precisely because that discourse resists his insight. Yet, once we penetrate his special language, we discover to our astonishment that the insight is no more

7

complicated than a common-sense reading of experience. It is certainly not beyond the ken of ordinary people. In this regard it may be helpful to compare Levinas's work to Franz Rosenzweig's *Understanding the Sick and the Healthy*. Written at his publisher's request as a more popular version of his almost impenetrable book, *The Star of Redemption,* this book is a parable telling the story of a patient, "Sick Reason," who is cured by being increasingly exposed to the world of real experience. Rosenzweig decided at the last moment not to allow publication of the book (which was finally published by the Noonday Press in 1954, translated by Nahum Glatzer). The book demonstrates that the density of Rosenzweig's philosophical language does not preclude our understanding his thought. I believe that this is true of Emmanuel Levinas's work as well.

Although I do not propose to write such a parable for Emmanuel Levinas, I do believe that we can appreciate his work if we understand that what he is describing is a reality. According to Levinas, experience precedes thought. This founding experience preceding all others is the experience of the other, that is, of other people outside ourselves. Our relationship to the other precedes thought, precedes our thought of ourselves, precedes our very idea of self. In fact, our sense of self arises from our relationship to another. We come into being because of another who, unbidden and inscrutable, tends to us. We are fundamentally beholden to this other person; regardless of our own will we are chosen by this indebtedness, "elected," as it were. We are created by another's love and create ourselves by accepting the burden of this love and its obligations. In short, what philosophers call ethics (what should be) not only precedes ontology (what is) but makes it possible. Before philosophy, there is responsibility.

This achievement of what Richard Cohen calls "an original, profound and comprehensive philosophy, a dialogical ethics," is, then, not nearly as mysterious as some claim. However, finding an appropriate philosophic language in which to translate this dialogical ethics is difficult. Yet so important and enlightening is the language that Levinas creates that it behooves all of us who live in a world created by Western philosophy to make the effort to understand it. I use the word "translate" deliberately, for Levinas's program should be understood as one of translation—in fact, of double translation. His insistence that we found all philosophy on ethical responsibility is, in effect, a translation of Jewish wisdom into the philosophic language of the West—that is, Greek thought. Conversely, his readings of Talmud constitute a translation of Greek modes of thought into the foundational language of Judaism, for to search within the Talmud for its implicit principles in order to articulate those principles is nothing short of an act of cultural translation. Levinas himself calls his philosophic program the creation of a "septuagint," referring to the original translation of the Hebrew Bible into Greek.

I began by introducing you to Levinas through the dedications of his two great works. But *Otherwise Than Being or Beyond Essence* has a second dedication. What I quoted above was the English translation of the French dedication. There is also a Hebrew dedication in which Levinas dedicates the book specifically to his father, his mother, his brothers, and his in-laws, but in the Hebrew there is no mention of the rest of the victims, only of those who were very much "closest." Levinas chose this second dedication in Hebrew because he wanted the specificity of that language. He needed both languages because in translation the specific inevitably becomes more general, more philosophical.

In order to understand Levinas's septuagint and to profit from the nuances that every translation inevitably adds to the original, I propose to investigate a series of crucial Levinasian terms. What follows is a sort of Levinasian dictionary that will serve as an introduction to and explication of Levinas's work.

TIME, LOVE, AND FECUNDITY

Time, in the Levinasian world, is a function of our relationship with another. Levinas is not referring to our varied personal experiences of time nor to our artificial ways of "chopping up" time into discrete units. Rather, he claims to be able to describe time itself. In order to do so, and to prove that time is "the very relationship of the subject with the Other"(*TO,* p. 39), Levinas first describes and explores solitude, for, to construct a relationship between ourselves and another, we must first study the self, separate from the other.

Prior even to our studying the self, and necessary for us fully to understand its characteristics, Levinas asks: How does the self, an "existent," come out of the flow of existence-as-such? That is, how does an individual emerge from eternal being, a finite differentiated being from the infinity of the "there is"? Levinas calls this "rupture" breaking out of the anonymity of being, consciousness. When someone becomes conscious, that person is differentiated from being-as-such. Levinas calls this process "hypostasis." Each conscious being is first alone, existing in solitude. That so many other beings are also alone does not alter the solitude of each. He writes, "One can exchange everything between beings except existing," and, perhaps more poignantly, "I touch an object, I see the other, but I am *not* [emphasis original] the other. I am all alone."

Levinas posits that "materiality and solitude go together." We can exist to and for ourselves only embodied, concerned with our physical selves. For Levinas, consciousness can occur only in a material being, what he calls an existent. Thus, we live in the world, the real world of everyday life, as beings characterized by our solitude and our materiality.

Therefore, an individual's primary occupation is taking care of himself or herself. Yet, our concern with our own materiality makes us profoundly unhappy. For to be alone in the world is to be profoundly unhappy. As it says in Genesis: "It is not good for the man to be alone" (2:18). And yet, living in the everyday life of the world moves us away from solitude, begins to drive a wedge between the self and its sole identification with itself. Everyday life provides us an escape from our initial solitude. Levinas calls this characteristic of everyday life a preoccupation with salvation. It is in the world that the demands of self first confront the presence of others. It is in the world that we act, ultimately enjoying the objects and subjects in the world with whom we act. Acting in the world, enjoying the world, breaches our solitude slightly. But because we start with ourselves and view ourselves as the object of our own vision, we are still left alone. Neither our material pursuits nor the light of reason can free us from this solitude.

Since we cannot disentangle our self from our ego by merely satisfying our material needs—since we always come back to ourselves—then something must arise to interrupt our solitude. This "something" is suffering. That is, the work of our being in the world produces in the end a profound pain, physical and moral. ("By the sweat of your brow/ Shall you get bread to eat . . . " [Gen. 3:19]). Moral pain is produced by our inability to overcome our solitude. More important, for Levinas, however, is his belief that our pursuit of happiness—that is, our effort to satisfy our material needs—inevitably produces physical pain and suffering:

In pain and suffering, we once again find, in a state of purity, the finality that constitutes the tragedy of solitude. The ecstasis of enjoyment does not succeed in surmounting this finality. (*TO,* pp. 68–69)

In suffering there is an absence of all refuge. It is the fact of being directly exposed to being. It is made up of the impossibility of fleeing or retreating. The whole acuity of suffering lies in this impossibility of retreat. It is the fact of being backed up against life and being. In this sense suffering is the impossibility of nothingness. (*TO,* p. 69)

Suffering "backs us up" against that which we cannot know, cannot make into ourselves. It confronts us with a mystery which is neither nothing nor identical with us. That mystery is death. In our encounter with death, presaged by suffering, we lose all mastery; we are entirely passive. Death lies beyond the light of our reason. It cannot be dismissed as "nothing," yet it is unknowable. This is why Levinas writes: "Death is never a present." It is eternally future for us. Because death is absolutely other, we cannot assimilate it into ourselves through work or enjoyment, and therefore it does not confirm our individual solitude but, rather, breaks it. Death, which occurs one life at a time, confirms that existence is plural, that another person is in no way another myself.

> The relationship with the other is not an idyllic and harmonious relationship of communion, or a sympathy through which we put ourselves in the other's place; we recognize the other as resembling us, but exterior to us; the relationship with the other is a relationship with a Mystery. (*TO*, p. 75)

The Mysterious Other can never be in the present for us. Our relationship to it is always in the future. Because we can never really know another as we know ourselves, others remain a surprise to us. While death can never be a present for us, suffering, which gives us our first hint of death, can be. The intuition of our death, which suffering allows us, is an intuition of the future. Time is impossible for the solitary individual. Rather we experience time in the quality of the relationship between ourselves and the mysterious other who breaks our solitude, for whom we suffer and whose death threatens to annihilate us.

However, the arrival of time in the form of death, while philosophically interesting, does not explain how we can experience time in life. Levinas poses the question: "How can a being enter into relation with another without allowing itself to be crushed by that other?" He calls this the question of "the preservation of the ego in transcendence."

> The future that death gives, the future of the event, is not yet time. In order for this future, which is nobody's and which a human being cannot assume, to become an element of time, it must also enter into a relationship with the present. (*TO*, p. 79)

This relationship is both other and present, unknowable, inassimilable, surprising, and oriented toward the future. This relationship is what we generally call history. Time is fundamentally a function of the relationship between oneself and another. And when we draw near one another without annihilating our individual selves, we are in the presence of love.

Thus, for Levinas as for Rosenzweig before him, love is as strong as death, as the Bible maintains (Songs 8:6). Love derives its strength from our ability to form a relationship with another, each of us entirely mysterious, unknowable to each other, each of us intact in our individual identities. Here is a relationship that does not require my death. This relationship is characterized by modesty and unfolds outside the light of knowledge, for love is not a knowledge, is not susceptible to reason any more than death is. And it does not require that I forfeit my ego. As Levinas writes, "Love is not a possibility, is not due to our initiative, is without reason; it invades and wounds us, and nevertheless the I survives it" (*TO,* pp. 88–89).

Although death provides us with a horizon we call the future, we cannot live in its temporal framework because we cannot survive our relationship with it. But we can survive and sustain our relationship with love; for, when we love another, our ego survives. The future that death only promises becomes a reality through love.

When we are in a loving relationship with another, we are brought closer to time as we actually experience it. However, we face another danger. Just as death threatens the annihilation of our individual selves, so too love threatens a similar loss as we surrender ourselves to another. How can I, in love, establish a relationship with another who allows me to return to myself? Levinas here introduces a third kind of relationship, one characterized by what he calls "fecundity." When we are in a relationship with our child we are connected to someone who is both part of ourselves and a mysterious other. Thus, our child is both our future and his/her own.

Paternity is not simply the renewal of the father in the son and the father's merger with him, it is also the father's exteriority in relation to the son, a pluralist existing. (*TO,* p. 92)

This is Levinas's goal: to explain the presence of another for whom I am responsible and who breaks my solitude and thereby breaks the solitude of being as mistakenly described by Western philosophy. Levinas wants to establish a plurality in being which still allows room for my ability to maintain my individual integrity.

The shock of recognition reading Levinas is thus twofold. First, the cogency with which he describes a reality is much more compelling than that reality described by the main lines of Western philosophy. Second, for a Jew conversant with Jewish language, the language of the Bible and Talmud, reading Levinas is like reading a masterful translation of a text which one knows in the original but now comes to know again in all its beauty because of the power of the translation. Learning again about the victory of love over death, rediscovering the mysteriousness of another, has taught me to listen better to the sources of Jewish wisdom brought to life in Levinas's translation of those sources from Hebrew into Greek.

THE FACE, THE TRACE, AND THE THIRD PERSON

Levinas structures time through love and death. Complementing one another, love and death provide the basis for understanding solitude and the interruption of solitude by another. However, further analysis is required so that we can understand our lives in the context of time. In the course of this analysis of our lives, Levinas returns us to the dynamics of the meeting between the one person and another.

Each of us is initially concerned with his or her own physical needs. Yet, when our needs are fulfilled, we uncover the profound unhappiness that Levinas contends is the lot of isolated and self-interested people. In this discovery we find ourselves desiring another. This desire is not merely a bigger need but is qualitatively different from need. It demands a greater effort that is never exhausted but from which we never seek relief.

This person who interrupts my self-absorption while remaining a mystery to me faces me with all of his or her needs and enigmas, and, according to Levinas, commands me. When I look at the face of another and instead of seeing myself I see his or her needs, my self-absorption is finally interrupted. The only way I can, in good faith, respond to those needs is to serve them. The other person's face obligates me. Remarkably, this obligation coincides with my own desire to serve another, which grows stronger the more it serves. For Levinas, this is the meaning of consciousness itself. This is the context in which we live as individuals separated from the anonymous flow of being. Finding meaning in life comes not by analyzing anonymous being, what Levinas calls self-absorption, but by allowing someone else to interrupt the anonymity of being. That "something" is the face of another. This definition of meaning emphasizes Levinas's goal of providing a definition that goes beyond that of standard philosophies, a meaning predicated on "something" beyond being, "the good beyond being"—that is, ethics.

Our responsibility to each other in all our mystery leads Levinas selectively to incorporate into the philosophic discourse words and phrases taken from the biblical tradition. The response of serving the needs of another he calls our "election." In his terms, we are elected as "our brother's keeper." He speaks of our ability to say "Here I am" to the other, as a way of establishing our presence in history. He defines history as time that elapses in the course of my meeting my responsibilities to another in whose very face I read the first and, in Levinas's view, the most powerful of commandments: "Thou shalt not murder."

Here I want to recall the shock of recognition that occurred when I first read these ideas in Levinas's work. Was he not describing the Judaism that I always knew? Was he not translating the stories of creation and revelation into a language characterized by the use of phrases like "the interruption in pure being by the commanding other"? Wasn't this language of responsibility precisely the language of Abraham's struggle on behalf of the innocent people of Sodom and Gomorrah? Wasn't Levinas translating the most profound insights discovered through the People of Israel's ongoing encounter with the mystery of the other into a language amenable to "Greek" readers? As we shall see below, this claim is borne out by the number of specific Judaic texts that Levinas explicates: Bible, Talmud, the writings of Rabbi Hayyim of Volozhin. But when he draws from them precisely these ideas that he has described in his general philosophy, he makes few if any references to Judaic tradition. Reading Levinas, I discovered another Jewish text, one written in translation, but a translation not literally from the Hebrew language to the Greek language, but of Hebrew thought to Greek thought.

INFINITY

Before we return to the subject of the face, we are at this point drawn to look more closely at the subject of infinity and its juxtaposition with the idea of totality in Levinas's central work *Totality and Infinity.* I have thus far purposely avoided using the word "infinity." We have come to understand that the problem of totality, the problem bequeathed by Rosenzweig to Levinas and that both thinkers identified as the problem *par excellence* of Western thinking from Parmenides to Heidegger, is none other than our inability to respond to the face of another. On the contrary, the thrust of Western thought is to see, pre-eminently, the reflection of ourselves in the face of another.

What we have called being-in-general, or the flow of being, is to be distinguished from *a* being, our being, by consciousness. The meaning of that consciousness is located in its ability to see another who interrupts its solitude with a glance. In this glance, in the face of another, we recognize, if only fleetingly, what Levinas calls a "trace." The trace is a memory of being-in-general, of the infinite. It is a memory of a past we cannot have experienced, for "we" can only exist as creatures separate from the infinite. Nevertheless, we recognize the infinite, recall it. The other person and the infinite Other that is never present for us reveal themselves together in the human face. There is, thus, in every meeting between two people, a third person: a trace of the Infinite, a memory of an always absent past. The other person and the Other face me together. They face no one else at that moment. Be it in a smile, a sigh, or a tear, they *open* themselves to me, and I cannot in conscience turn away—I am chosen at that moment. Like it or not, I must respond. The nature of that response will occupy us next.

THE RESPONSE TO THE FACE: LANGUAGE AND ETHICS

The face of another communicates to me. It expresses itself, and this expression cannot be avoided. It commands me, "Thou shalt not murder." It expresses, also, its pressing needs, and in doing so, obligates me. In *Totality and Infinity*, Levinas directly quotes the Talmud but once:

"To leave men without food is a fault that no circumstance attenuates; the distinction between the voluntary and the involuntary does not apply here," says Rabbi Yoḥanan. (*TI*, p. 201, citing Sanhedrin 201b)

Levinas uses this Talmudic statement to introduce and emphasize the ethical imperative that lies behind language.

Our response to another's face is speech. Language, itself the very heart of reason, begins as an ethical commitment. Before it communicates any content, language responds to the expression of the face. As a response to the face of another, language is an expression of that "here I am" that we spoke of earlier, one of the biblical ideas Levinas is attempting to convey. As such, language bears witness to our personal presence. The beginning of intelligibility, of rational discourse, is our spoken response to the command of another. Because the expression of the other person commands me, Levinas speaks of that expression as coming from above me, like a sovereign. Once more there is a hint of biblical imagery.

Language does much more than foster communication between us. In fact, communication occurs before language. Language witnesses our presence for each other in response to the expression on each of our faces. It is a form of communication, a first gesture of ethics. "Here I am," the phrase of Abraham, Isaac, and Jacob, sums up the first principle of speech. We are here for each other/Other. We are here both for the other person and the trace of the third person present in every face-to-face encounter.

Critical to the primacy of language as a first gesture of ethics is the fact that language, in Levinas's analysis, is public. Because language is a public gesture, Levinas does not accept the definition of a relationship between one person and another in terms of the "I–Thou" that characterized Martin Buber's well-known philosophy. Levinas rejects language that becomes entirely private, what he calls "the self-sufficient 'I–Thou' forgetful of the universe." Instead, he claims that every time two people look into one another's faces, the eyes of other people are also, as it were, present. When we look at each other we cannot see only each other, but all those others who also demand our ethical attention. Levinas writes: "The third party looks at me in the eyes of the Other—language is justice." The third *person* revealed in the face of the other—the trace of infinity—simultaneously testifies to the presence of a third *party.*

It is the public nature of language, the presence in language of a third party, that turns every meeting between one person and another into a meeting that must include the whole of humanity. "I–Thou" is transformed into "We–Thou." The creation through language of the "we" permits the existence of human community, fraternity, and the equality of that community—equally part of the "We" before the "Thou." Thus, because language is a public phenomenon, it contains my response and responsibility for another together with the response and responsibility of my brother or sister for that same face. Each of us must witness the trace of the Other revealed in the face. Language takes shape in the form of a commandment and therefore founds the discourse of justice.

AN INTERRUPTION: LEVINAS AND TALMUD

Although my presentation of a Levinasian dictionary is not complete, I feel compelled to interrupt this systematic progression. As we have already seen, for Levinas one of the most significant failings of Western philosophy is its dependence on the creation of total systems. Therefore, in his own work, both philosophic and talmudic, he practices a kind of self-interruption in order to avoid a similar failing. I too will occasionally interrupt my narrative in order to allow the growth of an alternate, whose counterpoint is crucial to the meaningfulness of both stories.

I interrupt my narrative about Levinas's work at this point because we have come to the juncture of language and justice. Thus far we have defined discourse as the unfolding of language—the bastion of reason—toward a simultaneously personal and universal other "faced" by a fraternal "we." This phenomenon parallels the work of the Talmud too closely to ignore. Where else but in the Talmud do we encounter a language so devoted to finding justice in every mundane situation, so committed to finding out exactly what we are commanded to do in the face of others? Where else is our being commanded as a "we," a fraternal community "elected" to respond to the commandments of the Other, taken so for granted?

Let's begin by looking at Levinas's essay "Spinoza's Background" in the collection *Beyond the Verse*. Here Levinas is relatively loquacious regarding his own understanding of talmudic principles. Although he does not directly discuss either his readings of the talmudic texts or principles derived from Mr. Chouchani, he systematically presents his own view of the Talmud in his attempt to prove that Spinoza would not have dismissed rabbinic biblical commentary had he been familiar with the Talmud.

Regarding the Talmud's use of scripture Levinas writes:

> What is sought after, and often achieved, in the incessant return to verses by the Talmudic scholars . . . , which indeed does end up in multiple interpretations that apparently move away from the plain meaning, is a reading where the passage commented upon clarifies for the reader its present preoccupation (which may be either out of the ordinary or common to its generation), and where the verse, in its turn, is renewed in the light of this clarification. (*BTV*, p. 170)

In other words, the Talmud "reads" Scripture in order to clarify its own contemporary questions. To do so requires multiple interpretations that *apparently* move away from the plain meaning of the scriptural text. What does Levinas mean by the word "apparently"? He is quite strongly suggesting that these multiple interpretations constitute the *plain* meaning of the text, not its elaboration. Levinas expands on this idea as his essay continues:

> Exegesis would be the possibility for one epoch to have a meaning for another epoch. In this sense, history is not something that relativizes the truth of meaning. The distance that separates the text from the reader is the space in which the very evolution of the spirit is lodged. Only this distance allows meaning to mean fully and to be renewed. In the light of exegesis, then, one may speak of continuous Revelation, as one speaks in theology and philosophy of continuous Creation. (*BTV*, p. 170)

After this essential paragraph come references to the three rabbinic stories to which Levinas alludes almost every time he touches upon his method of talmudic interpretation. The first is the story of Moses, who, wanting to know the future of the Torah, is transported to the academy of Rabbi Akiba, where he finds that what is being taught is incomprehensible to him. His melancholy is dispelled, however, when Rabbi Akiba ends his discourse by attributing all of what he has taught to what had been taught by Moses at Mount Sinai. The second is the story of a rabbinic dispute into which a heavenly voice brings a divine opinion, only to have it overruled, because the Torah is no longer in heaven and therefore not subject to heavenly jurisdiction. Finally, Levinas refers to the rabbinic analogy that the meaning of Torah is "like the hammer striking the rock and causing countless sparks to fly." These stories, already popular within the tradition, have become especially commonplace in critical studies of Talmud in the modern era. Here Levinas challenges us to go beyond mere historiography, to understand exegesis as the stuff of sacred history as well as mundane history. He calls this the "evolution of the spirit." But now he goes further, specifically placing responsibility for this evolution on every serious reader of the text:

Something would remain unrevealed in the Revelation if a single soul in its singularity were to be missing from the exegesis. That this process of renewal may be taken as alterations of the text is not ignored by the Talmudic scholars. (*BTV*, p. 171)

Before breaking off this interruption to return to a consideration of Levinas's philosophy, I will add a few last thoughts. First, what I have presented here forms the basis for many of my own principles of talmudic methodology discussed below—that is, Levinas's general remarks have become for me principles of interpretation. Second, I would like to point out that Levinas is struggling to present the Talmud to the world and to the Jewish people in their worldly—that is, Western, assimilated—status. His enterprise is, then, as I have contended, an act of double translation. Why? Susan Handelman suggests the following:

In sum, he is dissatisfied with the options contemporary thought has offered for a free, nondogmatic exegesis—options such as historicism, sociology, philology, or formalistic analyses. (*FOR*, pp. 308–309)

That is, Levinas wants to bring to the non-Jewish reader a new discourse in which totality is broken, in which reason is not abandoned but is founded on what is prior to reason—namely, ethics.

But what, then, does he want to bring to his Jewish readers? Levinas himself answers that question in a speech given at the Presidential Palace in Jerusalem on the subject of "Assimilation and New Culture." He claims that what he wants to bring to Jewish readers is a new/old way of reading Talmud through which Jews can discover a meaning in Jewish particularity, so that they can fill in the lacunae left by Western universalism—the lacunae of totalization, totalitarianism, and genocide.

Thus, the translation project is important for Jews and non-Jews alike. Levinas says:

For one would have every right to ask if this apparent limitation of universalism is not what protects it from totalitarianism; if it does not arouse our attention to the murmurs of inner voices; if it does not open our eyes to the faces which illuminate and permit the control of social anonymity, and to the vanquished of humanity's rational history where it is not just the proud who succumb. (*BTV*, p. 200)

Once more we encounter the force of the word "apparent." Is not its "apparent" limitation on universalism, Judaism's particularity, the true universalism? A universalism able to recognize its obligation to the other? A pluralist universalism? Of this particularism Levinas says:

But it is a peculiarity that the long history from which we are emerging has left in a state of sentiment and faith. It needs to be made explicit to thought. It cannot here and now provide educational rules. It still needs to be translated into the Greek language which, thanks to assimilation, we have learnt in the West. Our great task is to express in Greek those principles about which Greece knew nothing. Jewish peculiarity awaits its philosophy. The servile imitation of European models is no longer enough. The search for references to universality in our Scriptures and texts of the oral Law still come from the process of assimilation. These texts, through their two-thousand-year-old commentaries, still have something else to say. (*BTV*, pp. 200–201)

Thus we are brought back to exegesis, now as part of both sides of a double translation.

A SECOND INTERRUPTION: ḤAYYIM OF VOLOZHIN

One of the most influential Jewish texts to which Levinas makes frequent reference in his work is the book *Nefesh ha-ḥayyim*, "Soul of Life," by Rabbi Ḥayyim of Volozhin, also known as the Volozhiner. This text develops a theoretical structure to account for the primacy of Torah study in Jewish spirituality—a study not limited to the pursuit of knowledge but, rather, a fully articulated way of life. *Nefesh ha-ḥayyim* takes for granted our familiarity with biblical, talmudic, and kabbalistic texts and, what is more important, our willingness to be convinced by these texts.

Levinas presents the work as establishing "the meaning of the humanity of man in the general economy of creation." Before he does this, he describes what we could call its problems of translation: its lack of reference to Western philosophy and its dependence instead on Judaic texts. Specifically, the text's problem for us is the rabbinic mode of exegesis—midrash—"which solicits the letter of the text in order to seek out, above and beyond the plain meaning, the hidden and allusive meaning." Levinas expounds on the burdens of being a translator. Speaking to "ultra-moderns"—by which he could mean not only "postmoderns," but anyone prepared to think otherwise than in Greek—he writes, "We shall try to find in them [rabbinic texts] a vision of the human which is still meaningful today and, in some ways freed from its language of the time."

Our larger interest is in Levinas's attraction to the structure of Rabbi Ḥayyim's thought. For our purposes it can be summarized as a complex answer to three questions, whose combined power is extraordinary for Levinas:

1. What does it mean to be created in the image of God (*Elohim*)?
2. What is the meaning of God expressed by the term *Elohim* and how does it differ from the meaning expressed by the Tetragrammaton (YHVH)?
3. What is the relation of the *Ein Sof* (the Infinite, which cannot be named but can be "thought" as an "absolute which never reaches the absolute") and the God of religion?

Using a variety of rabbinic and kabbalistic sources, Rabbi Ḥayyim fleshes out an answer to these questions that goes further than his sources in placing on the shoulders of human beings the responsibility for the very maintenance of the universe. When the Torah speaks of creation in the image of *Elohim,* it is describing a creature to whom the "God of all powers," by a necessary act of love, gives over those very powers to humans. Our world, indeed all the worlds, which exist as higher degrees of emanation from the godhead and are closer, as it were, to the source, unfettered by materiality, are none the less dependent on the human, at once the lowest and the highest. Although every world is a lesser manifestation of the world above it, the world of humans both is and is not.

Let us see how this can be so. Each person contains a tripartite soul: *Nefesh* (creatureliness, animation), *Ruaḥ* (spirit or wind, consciousness), and *Neshamah* (divine breath, consciousness of self and the other). While the first two of these derive from the emanation of the godhead through the progressive weakening of its reach through the worlds, the third derives from the top directly—perhaps from even above the top itself. In relation to the godhead as *Elohim*—the God of All Powers—human beings share the same source. Human beings are the goal of creation, both its lowest or final level and its crowning achievement.

This "fact" has clear consequences for both Rabbi Ḥayyim and for Levinas. Levinas quotes the Volozhiner in two central statements:

His will, blessed be He, confers upon man the power to free or to stop ["to open and close"] thousands of myriads of forces and worlds, on account of all the detail and all the levels of his conduct and all his perpetual concerns, thanks to the superior root of his deeds, words and thoughts, as if man too were the master of the forces that command these worlds [parenthesis in original].(*BTV*, p. 160)

Levinas concludes, "This mastery is interpreted without hesitation as responsibility."

Let no one in Israel—God forbid!—say to himself: "What am I and what can I accomplish through my humble deeds in the world?" Let him understand, rather, let him know and let him fix in his thought that not one detail, from any moment at all, is lost of his deeds, words and thoughts. Each one goes right back to its root in order to carry on in the height of heights, in the worlds and among the pure superior lights. The intelligent man who understands this according to the truth will fear and tremble in his heart in thinking of the points reached by his bad deeds, of the corruption and destruction that even a slight misdeed may cause. . . . Let the heart of the holy people tremble, for it includes in its stature all the forces and all the worlds . . . for these are the holiness and the sanctuary above. . . . Just as the body's behaviour and movements are due to the soul that is inside man, man as a whole is the power and living soul of the upper and lower countless worlds which are all led by him. (*BTV,* p. 160)

Levinas continues, by way of drawing the obvious Jewish conclusion: "Consequently, the system of *mitzvot* acquires cosmic import in its universality, confirms its ethical significance: to practice the commandments is to endure the being of the world." He writes also: "In spite of his humility as a creature, man is either in the process of damaging or protecting the world."

Levinas concludes this analysis of the meaning of human beings in the economy of creation according to Rabbi Ḥayyim of Volozhin: "Man does not sin against God when he disobeys commandments; he destroys worlds" (*BTV,* p. 161).

The preceding analysis of people is in respect to the God *Elohim,* the God who is present in the world (or worlds) and who is concerned for our relations with others. Levinas quotes the Volozhiner in calling this the "God on our side." But there is also the "God on His own side," the God of the Tetragrammaton, "signifying something that man cannot define, formulate, think or even name." This is the *Ein Sof,* the Infinite. "What," asks Levinas, "does the human mean in relation to this new notion?" Returning to Rabbi Ḥayyim, Levinas analyzes this text from *Nefesh ha-ḥayyim:*

And even if the *Zohar* designates this essence by the name of *En-Sof* (Infinite), this is not a name. For this concerns only the way in which we reach it from out of the forces that have emanated from It, when It desires to associate itself with the worlds. This is why it is called *En-Sof* (endless) and not beginningless. For in reality, *on its own side,* it has neither end nor beginning, but our means of understanding its forces, our understanding is only a beginning; there is no end for the understanding that goes out to reach the forces emanated from it [parenthesis in original]. (*BTV,* p. 164)

And Levinas comments: "Strictly speaking, then, that which is infinite and never ending is not the absolute of God which nothing can determine, but the *act of thinking of the Absolute which never reaches the Absolute,* and this has its own way—which is quite something—of missing the Absolute." He claims that the text quoted above "suggests a beginning that does not move toward an end, but traces, as it were, a relation without a correlate. . . . The human, therefore, would not just be a creature to whom revelation is made, but something through which the absolute of God reveals its meaning."

We thus arrive at the answers to Rabbi Ḥayyim's three questions. More important, for our purposes, we understand the structure of thought and the wisdom that Levinas attributes to the talmudic tradition and its ancillary traditions, including Lurianic Kabbalah (of which Rabbi Ḥayyim is identified as a master who gives a clear and systematic elaboration of that tradition). Finally, it becomes clear that the primacy of ethics that Rabbi Ḥayyim demands—the world depends on it!—is bequeathed equally to the radical translator, Emmanuel Levinas.

Elohim is the God in being, the God whose terminus is in the same Absolute as ours and therefore whose very mission we share. The creation this God rules depends on our actions. However, this God is neither Infinite nor Absolute, any more than we are. The God of the Tetragrammaton, by contrast, cannot be thought or named but leaves a trace specifically in and through the human. This trace is left in the power that *Elohim* and man share—the Torah, which conjoins the Infinite, both *Elohim* and man, in law—that is, in commandments, in ethics, and in language— and which, as we shall see, precedes speech and is already absent from that which is said.

The beginning of communication, which is the beginning of responsibility, comes with the self's turning to the face of the other. The other's face reveals its expression, which thereby elects the self, and obligates one in a commanding moment. That expression "speaks" to us. It expresses its need in a not uncertain, nor ambiguous, "saying." A "word" unspoken, it is yet clearly heard by the one who turns to listen unafraid.

There is a story in the Hasidic literature: The tradition informs us that when the people Israel were gathered at the foot of Mount Sinai, the Presence of God, the first sound of God's voice, frightened them. They were unable to hear the entire revelation—all of the "ten words." After hearing the first commandment they fell back (some say they died and had to be resurrected!) and sent Moses ahead to hear the rest for them. Some say it was not the first commandment but only the first word of the first commandment. Still others maintain that it was only the first letter of the first word. What is that letter? The *alef.* What is its sound? The *alef* makes no sound! It is the beginning of speech, the sound of the breath at the start of speech—the moment between inspiration and aspiration. It is the "saying" of a word unspoken. When God spoke, only the *alef* was heard.

Words spoken such that they can be written are a person's response to the expression of the face of an other. The "saying" of that response is never quite captured in the "said" of writing. The "saying" is recoverable as an experience aided by language—but is absent from language *per se.* Yet, you and I need language—the "we" speaking to one another in the light of the "thou" require language. All of our language can potentially convey the "saying" behind the "said." All of our important language must try to do so—that is what makes it important, what makes it literature.

Our most important language—our Scriptures, our prophetic speeches, and our prayers—accomplish or come close to accomplishing the recovery of the "saying" in the "said." The Bible breaks up the "said" in order to recover the "saying" by means of its impossible chronology, its impossible burdens, and its impossible demands which the people Israel "do and then hear"—that is, they act in response to the commandments before expressing them in language. Midrash, the exegesis of the Bible, continues to break up the "said" and to recover the "saying" for any given moment. This establishes a new "said," the Law. We call the law the halakhah, the "way" of acting that best captures the "saying" of the "said" in society and in its institutions.

According to Levinas, in the Talmud "the problems it [the law] deals with are constantly under discussion. Its arguments conflict with one another, yet they remain, these and these alike, to use its own expression, 'the words of the living God'" (*BTV,* p. 169). The Talmud is thus the appropriate model of a discourse able to interrupt a philosophy that posits the totality of being. It thereby allows us to glimpse the Infinite that is traced before our eyes on the face of the other. It directs our vision *toward* the Infinite, *toward* God, who is otherwise than being, incomprehensible, absent, irrevocably past, and incontrovertibly future.

TOWARD GOD

God *is* never present. For neither "is-ness"—that is, being—nor presence—that is, time isolated from the relation to another person—can comprehend God. To put it more simply, we know nothing of God's being. Writes Levinas:

There can be no "knowledge" of God separated from the relationship with men. The Other is the very locus of metaphysical truth and is indispensable for my relation with God. He does not play the role of a mediator. The other is not the incarnation of God but precisely by his face, in which he is disincarnate, is the manifestation of the height in which God is revealed. (*TI*, p. 79)

The God of ontology is impossible.

In the first place, even to contemplate a God in being is to be forced to contemplate a God whose very being annihilates the self. Levinas refuses being to God. He requires, as it were, an atheism as the first step in going "toward God." Atheism establishes respect for human independence and dignity. Atheism is the recognition, using Rabbi Ḥayyim's kabbalistic terminology, that the Infinite has abandoned our world, the place where human life can exist (*tzimtzum*, or retraction, in Lurianic Kabbalah) and imbued the human with the power of the God of All Powers. But that is *in* being. Beyond, or otherwise than being, the Absolute, Infinite, God awaits—in the future.

As we have seen, this Infinite interrupts the totality of our enclosure in being, leaving, as it were, traces. The structure of time itself comes to us carrying traces of the Infinite on the human face. It is important to emphasize that God *is* not in the face of the other person, nor otherwise incarnate in another. Rather, the absence of God is palpable in the trace left on the face of another. Paradoxically, it is this palpable absence of

God traced in the face of another person that testifies to God's having passed this way.

God is not a being nor in being, but a "dimension" of experience. Richard Cohen writes in *Elevations:*

This is perhaps *the* central claim of all Levinas's thought, about which his entire work revolves: the face of the other manifests and is manifest in a moral height which is the dimension of G-d, the revelation of G-d. Prophecy, revelation, occurs between interlocutors. (*ELEV,* p. 183)

Faith will not bring us to this God beyond being, whose trace elevates the face of another above me, commanding me, and, with the face of the third party, demands justice. Neither unity with this God who passed by nor faith in his existence has meaning. Levinas writes:

The illeity of the excluded third party is not some kind of power of obliqueness refusing the straightforwardness of thematization and causality, and thus perhaps causing the eye to squint. Illeity, in an extremely specific way, is excluded from being, but orders it in relation to a responsibility, in relation to its pure passivity, a pure 'susceptibility': an obligation to answer preceding any questioning which would recall a prior commitment, extending beyond any question, any problem and any representation, and where obedience precedes the order that has furtively infiltrated the soul that obeys. Neither expected nor welcomed: the contrary would still be a near activity, an assumption; a 'traumatizing' order coming from a past that was never present, since my responsibility is answerable for the freedom of others. (*BTV,* p. 128)

I understand "illeity" as the philosophic equivalent of the Hebrew expression containing the letters Yud, Heh, Vav, Heh (YHVH), the Tetragrammaton, the "name" of God which is not a name, but a record of God's passing. The God YHVH, the God whose trace is illeity, is testified to by the language of human beings who are awakened by His passing and who, unable to sleep, experiencing what Levinas calls the insomnia of consciousness, are vigilant to the demands of His absence. Those demands, principally justice, cause us to renounce both the sleep of ontology—a philosophy of being—and religious ecstasy, both of which erase the distinction between time and infinity.

The world of the Bible is the world of time through which God has passed. It is a world always on this side of its final destination that has looked from afar and remembers the contours of that destination. The world of the Talmud is the world of time, of exile, a longing for a home always future yet remembered from the past. That home is a land from which we are perpetually taking leave. It is a world perpetually in search of justice through dialogue. Without law there can be no justice, but finding the law requires a dialectic unable to conclude itself. The law is known only in retrospect. We can say what it was, but not what it is or what it will be. The world of the Talmud is not eternal, but perpetually in time, calling us back to time and, therefore, toward God.

2

METHOD

METHOD: GENERAL REMARKS

My reading of the Talmud is best described as imaginative. By this I mean that I try to be as sensitive as I can be to the images, ideas, random thoughts, reactions, even distractions that occur as I read and, especially, talk about a text. "Talking" the text of the Talmud is all-important, an accepted principle of talmudic study for as long as it has proceeded. I make note of questions. Questions are wondrous. It is through the asking of questions that I enter the very fabric of the Talmud, which is, after all, a text that propels itself by way of questions. If it is possible to recover what Levinas calls the "saying" behind the "said," to return to the text as an oral tradition without abandoning the written form, to be in the presence of the original voices, then it is by way of asking questions. The dialectic—orality and the *shakla ve-taryia,* "question and answer"—has been the age-old method of the study of Talmud. It is this that I can imagine Mr. Chouchani emphasizing with Levinas and it is, to some extent, the teaching of Mr. Chouchani that I am trying to tease out of Levinas's work. However, my method is not limited to asking questions, and certainly not to asking questions "permitted" by the tradition.

An example: In the discussion of a *baraita,* material contemporaneous with the Mishnah but not in the Mishnah found at the beginning of the second chapter of the Talmudic tractate *Makkot,* Rabba says:

I would suggest that it is to meet such cases as when he intended to kill an animal, but killed a man; to kill a heathen, but killed an Israelite; to kill a premature-born, but killed a fully developed infant.

The context of this discussion is the question of who must flee to a city of refuge, who is free from all responsibility for an accidental murder, and who is considered totally responsible for an accidental murder because it is close enough to murder to be considered murder. Rabba concludes that all of the cases he mentions belong in the third category. Although we can think of circumstances in which it is clearly permitted to kill an animal, and even those in which it would be permitted to kill a premature infant, we would be unlikely to countenance the killing of a heathen. But we have to conclude that the Talmud imagines conditions in which it is permissible to kill a heathen. At the least, it is clear that a heathen does not have the same status of humanity as a Jew.

I ask myself whether the Talmud could indeed hold such a position. I allow myself to be troubled. To accommodate my discomfort, I rearrange my reading of the text to include this question. I also allow that this inequality in status between the heathen and the Israelite may be disquieting to the Talmud as well. It may even turn out that this question is a central motif of the *sugya* (unit of talmudic discussion). Because the practice of Talmud study is one that connects me to an ongoing tradition in which I do not have to rediscover every question on my own, I am certainly anxious to find support for my question in the traditional Talmudic commentaries—in Rashi, Tosafot, Ritba, Meiri, Rabbi Hananel—or in the various codes. But if I don't find such support, my question remains. It becomes part of my reading, part of the reading of someone who lives in a century characterized by the illusion that it is permissible to kill the "other." My question stands even if it is never answered. And since my reading is generally carried out in a group, with a partner or in a class or congregation, my question becomes part of the oral tradition, and in that way, part of the Talmud.

Traditionalists might argue that, in fact, the soul of the Jew is on a higher level than that of a gentile, just as the soul of a human being is higher than that of an animal. I demur. It is axiomatic in my method that in its orality, its original "saying," the Talmud resonates with the encounter between God and humans at Sinai; I am unable to conceive of that encounter establishing such a hierarchy. On the contrary, it is just that encounter which makes such a hierarchy ludicrous. Levinas reads every mention of "Israelite" in the Talmud as meaning "human being."

Although historians might argue that the Talmud's sensibility arises from a more primitive cultural milieu, from a time when it was more acceptable morally to view heathens as less human than Jews, I ask myself: Isn't such a view still possible, even today? And haven't there always been those who protest such a sensibility? Is it not this protest—the voice of Abraham arguing with God for the lives of the heathen citizens of Sodom and Gomorrah—that may well be the very Voice expressed by the Talmud text?

Asking questions such as these, however, is only one of the steps in my method. Derived from my reading of both the talmudic commentaries and philosophy of Emmanuel Levinas, I follow other steps, including using images, ideas, random thoughts, reactions, even distractions that occur during reading. These techniques are demonstrated in my Talmud readings below. They are, ultimately, intuitive and imaginative. In an interview given by Emmanuel Levinas to Salomon Malka in 1981, Levinas described the methodology of his own teacher, Mr. Chouchani: "He thought that one did not have to construct nor speculate abstractly, but through the imagination. One must think of those worlds evoked by each image of the text; it is then that the text begins to speak" (unpublished translation by David Harrington).

I approach the Talmud, as I believe Levinas does, in the same way that Buber and Rosenzweig approached the translation of the Hebrew Bible—as a unity. Buber wrote concerning their method:

All its stories and songs, all its sayings and prophecies are united by one fundamental theme: the encounter of a group of people with the Nameless Being whom they, hearing his speech and speaking to him in turn, ventured to name; their encounter with him in history, in the course of earthly events. ("People Today and the Jewish Bible")*

Jews have understood the Talmud to be a co-equal account of this encounter. Through its study, we encounter the Nameless Being in history and even more radically in the course of earthly, very earthly, events.

I bring these general remarks to a close with a summary list of principles. Before we practice the art of reading Talmud in detail, it is useful to understand the assumptions that guide my method. The fundamental principle is reported by Levinas in the name of his teacher, Chouchani: "One does not have to construct nor speculate abstractly, but through imagination." On this are based the following assumptions:

1. Reading Talmud requires sensitivity to images, ideas, reactions, random thoughts, even distractions, that occur in the process of reading.
2. Reading Talmud requires asking questions, permitted or not.

Martin Buber, "People Today and the Jewish Bible: From a Lecture Series," in Martin Buber and Franz Rosenzweig, *Scripture and Translation,* trans. Lawrence Rosenwald with Everett Fox (Bloomington: Indiana University Press, 1994).

3. The Talmud should be read aloud to approximate an oral tradition.
4. The Talmud is to be taken as a whole.
5. The Talmud is part of the story of the encounter between Israel and the "Nameless Being." This encounter precludes a sensibility of oppression.
6. Although historical and scientific information is essential for a proper reading of the Talmud, such information must be subject to the same images, ideas, reactions, random thoughts, even distractions and—especially—questions as the text.
7. The mention of "Israel" means human being. As Levinas wrote:

> Each time Israel is mentioned in the Talmud one is free, certainly, to understand by it a particular ethnic group which is probably fulfilling an incomparable destiny. But to interpret in this manner would be to reduce the general principle in the idea enunciated in the talmudic passage, would be to forget that Israel means a people who has received the Law and, as a result, a human nature which has reached the fullness of its responsibilities and of its self-consciousness . . . the heirs of Abraham are all nations; any man truly man is no doubt of the line of Abraham. (*NTR*, pp. xxix–xxx)

IN THE BEGINNING

The practice of Talmud begins by finding a suitable environment in which to read it. A variety of such environments exists, and no one is necessarily superior. Traditionally, three methods have been practiced: reading with a *ḥevruta* or study partner; attending a *shi'ur* or lecture-class; hearing a *vort* or *devar Torah,* a teaching shared at a community event ranging from a Bar/Bat Mitzvah to the anniversary of the death of a loved one, a *yahrzeit.* All these are potentially suitable environments for reading and expounding Talmud. All provide the opportunity for reading the text aloud. Even when studying alone, reading the text aloud is preferable to silent reading.

In what language should one read? Although it is certainly an advantage to read in the original language, since the nuances of the Aramaic/Hebrew text cannot be overestimated, even those familiar with Aramaic and Hebrew can benefit from using a translation. In fact, since almost no one has been able to claim Aramaic as a mother tongue since the close of the talmudic period itself, all Talmud reading has been an effort in translation. Reading Talmud is translating Talmud. The use of a variety of translations can be a helpful measure toward understanding. If one is familiar with the original language, the translation then becomes part of the argument.

If one is not, then the variety of translations opens up, at least, a range of possibilities for the reader to consider—that is to say, the Hebrew and Aramaic vocabulary of any specific talmudic discussion tends to be limited. By using the available dictionaries and translations, the reader can gain a reasonably accurate sense of the range of possible meanings of the main terms of the debate. The distinctions in the translations often indicate the particular interpretive stance of the translator and reflect, in turn, the translator's choice between alternative interpretations within the tradition. In this way, the reader of a translation enters into the same debates that take place in the original.

A final consideration vis-à-vis the environment is the most difficult to address. Much of the Talmud consists of legal argumentation. Although the text will often not take a final position on what the law is, it will always assume that its legal rulings are important to you, the reader, as a law-abiding, or as we say, an observant, Jew. That is, the Talmud is addressed to Jews for whom the yoke of the commandments is real, and while your stance toward the law should not logically affect your reading of the text, reading the Talmud is not merely a matter of logic. Knowing that the outcome of a particular discussion might very well determine how you act in the world has an effect on the reader. The text demands that level of seriousness, real-life seriousness. Although it is not always possible to read the text at this level of practical seriousness, it is preferable.

And now you are ready for the reading. The first reading. At the heart of my practice of Talmud is the regimen of three separate and complete readings of each *sugya.* An explanation of this practice will occupy the rest of these remarks. Before that, however, we must define a few terms.

The Talmud is divided into two parts. The first is the Mishnah. The Mishnah is a code of Jewish law that took its final form around the year 200 C.E. under the editorship of Rabbi Judah ha-Nasi in Israel. It is written in Hebrew and divided into six divisions called *sedarim,* or "orders." Each *seder* is further divided into *masekhtot* (singular, *masekhet*), or tractates. Each tractate is divided into chapters and each chapter into individual paragraphs called *mishnayot.* (The word *mishnah* thus can refer either to an individual unit or to the entire corpus of these units. In this book, "Mishnah" is capitalized when it refers to the entire corpus and begins with a lower-case *m* when it refers to an individual unit.)

Around each chapter of mishnah the Talmud or Gemara is constructed. The Gemara is a commentary on the Mishnah, paragraph by paragraph. It was written between the third and the sixth centuries in two versions—one written in Israel, the other in Babylonia. Both versions are written in Aramaic. We will be dealing only with the Babylonian Talmud, which is authoritative in Jewish tradition. Since the words "Gemara" and "Talmud"—both words having to do with learning—can be used interchangeably, we will use them in the following way: When we are discussing a literary unit containing both a mishnah and its Aramaic commentary, we will call it Talmud; when we are dealing only with that commentary itself, we will refer to it as gemara. In this book, "Gemara" is capitalized when it refers to the entire corpus and begins with a lower-case *g* when it refers to the commentary on an individual mishnah.)

A *sugya* is a cohesive unit of text in the Gemara, a single argument or a series of connected arguments on, broadly speaking, the same subject. Knowing where a *sugya* begins and ends is sometimes very easy. For example, when the discussion of a single subject is sustained between two *mishnayot,* the *sugya* begins with one mishnah and ends before the second mishnah. Sometimes, however, defining and delimiting the *sugya* is itself part of the process of interpretation. It is, in fact, often the reader's first intuitive act, the basis for the interpretation itself. What the reader deems germane or ungermane to a subject will set the boundaries of the *sugya* and materially affect that reader's interpretation of it. And because the text is a unity, a *sugya* is, in the long run, not an independent entity but part of a whole into which the *sugya* must fit. This whole is neither univocal nor consistent. Thus it is possible for one *sugya* to contradict another, and such a contradiction does not necessarily invalidate the conclusions regarding the first *sugya.* In the end, the *sugya* represents both a convenient way of chopping up the text and, at the same time, a single voice in a much larger, sometimes discordant, chorus.

THE FIRST READING

The purpose of the first reading is, simply put, to learn what's going on in the talmudic text, which is written in a stenographic language, a shorthand, perhaps even a code. The experienced reader learns to recognize a series of technical terms that have developed over time and that clue the reader into a wide range of information. These include terms that signal various types of questions or objections based either on textual controversies, logical disagreements, philosophic disagreements, or contradictions with other authoritative sources. The technical terms indicate the layers of the argumentation—that is, whether a challenge to a given statement is made on the basis of a contemporary source, an earlier source, or a later source. It is not always easy to ascertain what objection is being made to a statement, what its basis is, and whether it is sustained. The entire architecture of argument must be arranged in the reader's ear and mind before more substantive questions can be asked. Since it is almost impossible to explain this process, I propose to choose a very short sample *sugya* and work through it with you. I shall translate the passage into as literal an English as possible. Keep in mind that in its printed version the Talmud, like all ancient Hebrew and Aramaic texts, does not distinguish between what we call capital and lower-case letters. It contains no vocalization and no punctuation. In this first reading I will attempt to reproduce this effect in my translation. The lack of these sense-aids makes it all the more clear why reading the text aloud is essential. The inflection of the human voice brings the text into being. Every pause becomes a comma or period; questions and exclamations must be communicated by inflection.

40

The passage below is from the first chapter of Tractate *Megillah* in the Babylonian Talmud. It appears on pages 2b–3a, and is the second in a series of statements reported in the name of Rabbi Yirmeyah, or some say, Rabbi Ḥiyya bar Abba. The statements themselves are, at first blush, unrelated, connected only by the names of the teachers.

and said rabbi yirmeyah and/or if you say rabbi ḥiyya bar abba *mem nun tzadi peh kaf* seers said and if you will reason and its written these are the commandments that a prophet is not permitted to make new a thing/word from now and further rav ḥisda said *mem* and *samekh* of the tablets were standing by a miracle yes they existed and/but they didn't know which were middle of a word letters and which were end of a word and the seers came and fixed open ones in the middle of a word and closed at the end of a word finally these are the commandments that a future prophet will not make new a thing/word from now rather they forgot and returned and established

How impenetrable! Thus, the first reading of this text in any language requires an act of translation. Simply to divide it into sentences, to tease out the implications of some of the technical words used to frame the dialectic, often by inflection, is an interpretive act. But the passage is not as chaotic as it might appear. There are, after all, conventions of language that make this passage much more immediately understood by the native reader, and other conventions of technical language become second nature to the practiced reader. Yet, even with these conventions, this fairly simple passage opens a variety of questions that become apparent in the act of sorting out its surface meaning. I call these questions *anomalies*. During each reading of any text, including the first, I and my study partners keep a pad of paper on which to note both questions about the simple sense of the text and also these anomalies.

Since reading the text in such undifferentiated form as I have presented is never done in practice, let me mark up the passage so that it is at least readable at a basic level:

Rabbi Yirmeyah said, and some say it was Rabbi Ḥiyya bar Abba: the form of the Hebrew letters *mem, nun, tzadi, peh,* and *kaf* were instituted by the Prophets. Is this reasonable? But it is written in the Torah: "These are the commandments," teaching that a prophet is not permitted to introduce anything new from now on. And further, Rabbi Ḥisda said that the letters *mem* and *samekh* of the Tablets of the Law stood in place only by a miracle. Yes, they existed, but they did not know which form was to be used in the middle of a word and which at the end of a word, and the Prophets came and established that the open forms are to be used in the middle and the closed form at the end. Still and all, there is "These are the commandments," teaching that from now on no prophet will introduce anything new? Rather, they had forgotten, and they came and established them.

Our first reading of the Talmud, proceeding with this already somewhat interpreted text as its basis, is aimed at making certain that the simple argument being made here is understood by all. There is a traditional teaching that the forms of certain Hebrew letters—those that have two forms: one for use in the middle of a word and a different one for use at the end of a word—were established by the Prophets. But in this passage, this teaching is challenged. We discuss the challenge because the text uses the word *ve-tisb'ra* from the root *samekh-bet-resh*, meaning a tradition of reason or logic. Here is our first cue, a technical term that always indicates a challenge, often introduced from a traditional text or teaching and always extrapolated as a logical deduction from that text or teaching. In this case, the challenge arises from the Torah. We know this from our second cue, the technical term *ve-haktiv*, meaning, "and it is written." The Talmud text supplies the relevant quotation from the Torah. But the reader must realize that the key word in this quotation is "these." That is, *these* commandments written in the Torah—to the exclusion of all others—represent the entirety of God's teachings at Sinai. From this interpretation, Jewish tradition has deduced that no prophet after Moses may introduce anything new to the law.

But we are now faced with a contradiction: If this is the case, how could Rabbi Yirmeyah teach that the Prophets introduced the forms of the Hebrew letters in question? Furthermore, a second challenge is now offered. This challenge derives not from a *logical* contradiction but from a *physical* one: Rabbi Ḥisda claims that the letters *mem* and *samekh* remained on the two Tablets of the Law only by virtue of a miracle. Why? Because these two letters are entirely hollow, so that engraving them on the tablets would have pushed them out of the stone altogether. For the Midrash claims that the engraving is cut entirely through the tablets, so that the writing was visible from both sides. Since only the final form of *mem* would need a miracle to sustain it in place, the implication is that the final form of the *mem* was already used on the tablets and was therefore not introduced by the prophets. Convinced by this double-barreled challenge to the teaching of Rabbi Yirmeyah (or Rabbi Ḥiyya bar Abba), the gemara concludes that, in fact, the fixed form of the letters was already known before the Prophets came on the scene. The gemara now reframes the problem under discussion: By the time of the Prophets, it was not known for certain which form of these five letters should be used when. But now the gemara challenges itself. Even determining when to use which form constitutes introducing a new practice, which is expressly forbidden by the verse from the Torah. The argument is finally settled by the gemara's claim that this knowledge was known in the time of the Torah but was then forgotten. The Prophets thus only *re-discovered* it. Therefore, nothing new really happened. And here, our first reading ends.

THE SECOND READING

More often than not, the questions that are technically relevant to the second or third reading have already occurred and been asked during the first. But sometimes they have not. If new questions do arise, I ask people to write them down, to save them, to be certain that we understand the text before going off in other directions. We often do not understand the beginning of a discussion until we have worked through to its end. The second reading really has the same goal as the first but with greater confidence. In this regard, a second reading of our passage is not required. However, to give you some feeling for the types of issues that might be relevant in a typical second reading, I will ask a few questions concerning this passage which, although somewhat forced, might arise.

So we might first ask: Which forms of the letters *mem, nun, tzadi, peh,* and *kaf* are we referring to when we refer to the Prophets' innovations—the final or middle forms of the letters? How can it be claimed, to begin with, that the letters of the *alefbet* were not instituted until the time of the Prophets? Aren't all forms of the letters used in the written Torah? This question is, in fact, hinted at by the Tosafot, a school of medieval Talmud commentators, from whose comments here we learn that this question is, at first sight, even more complicated than we might have surmised. We also discover that the discussion that appears here in Tractate *Megillah* also appears in more elaborate form in Tractate *Shabbat.* There it is much clearer that Rabbi Ḥisda is referring to the closed, or what we call the final, letters. Knowing more about the context of Rabbi Ḥisda's statement forces us to reread the text. What, in our first reading and up to this point in our second reading, we read as two objections to Rabbi Yirmeyah turns out probably not to be two objections after all. So our second reading has, in fact, become a rereading.

In a second reading we might also begin to notice anomalies that arise in the text. In the case of our passage, these are readily apparent. First is the uncertainty of attribution. Does our passage begin with a teaching by Rabbi Yirmeyah or by Rabbi Ḥiyya bar Abba? Does it make a difference? To answer these questions, we would begin to research who these two sages were, which period they lived in, what their particular individual approach to the Torah was, based on their other appearances in the Talmud separately or together. Similarly, we would learn what we could about Rabbi Ḥisda. How does his statement here fit in with his larger body of material, his general *shita* (perspective) on matters of Torah? What is his relation with Rabbi Yirmeyah and Rabbi Ḥiyya? Did they live at the same time? If not, who might their opponents or audience have been in their own day? Were they talking about the same subject? If not, why does the gemara place them together? Does a particular "subtext" begin to emerge in which the gemara is raising other issues than those on the surface of the reading?

In the same vein, the center of this discussion is most certainly, from both a halakhic and a theological perspective, the question of changes instituted by the Prophets, and the subject of change in general. This leads us to ask questions concerning the choice of the word *tzofim* for "Prophets," rather than the usual *nevi'im*. Why does Rabbi Yirmeyah refer to the prophetic innovators as "the seers," and the gemara assume he meant "the Prophets"?

Thus, our second reading concludes. We have a clearer idea of what the text says. And we have, inevitably, begun to resonate to questions that are "outside" the text. Somewhere between the second and third reading, at the end of one and the beginning of the next, these questions begin to form a theme. In our sample passage the theme is easily identified: who can or cannot change the Torah tradition, who is or isn't a prophet, what is the difference between a (mere) seer and a prophet, and how does rabbinic authority fit into this picture? Although we do not know the outcome of the game, we have identified the players. In the third reading, which we typically begin with the theme in mind, we try to unravel the endgame.

THE THIRD READING

The third reading of the *sugya* builds on what has been learned from the first and second readings. The two "official" readings belie the number of times the text has literally been read. These prior readings now give birth to an imaginative reading, through which the reader discovers in the text its meaning in his or her own life as a participant in the discussion. Here is where practice metamorphoses into art.

Yet, though difficult to describe, this process is not so foreign or alien as it might appear. We experience it when we lift our eyes from the page of a book, seeing with our mind's eye ourselves as a character in the plot. It happens when the characters become familiar to us as friends and neighbors. It is that moment when the underlying intentions of the characters become clear despite the veil of their own language. This is when the reader can respond in love, distress, disgust, or sympathy to those intentions. Such a moment may be described as an experience of "normal mysticism," to adapt a phrase from my teacher, Rabbi Max Kadushin. Such moments are available to all of us.

The third reading involves an act of interpretation, when we freeze and study all our accumulated moments of imagination. Here, then, is the third reading of our sample passage: an interpretation.

THE FLOATING LETTERS OF THE COMMANDMENTS

In this passage it is very difficult to be certain who said what. A statement is reported in the name of Rabbi Yirmeyah. Or was it Rabbi Ḥiyya bar Abba? We're not sure. Since we are not sure, we are not free to decide but must faithfully report our uncertainty. But at the same time, we must faithfully respect the human particularity of the teaching by recognizing and remembering both of its possible authors.

Writing doesn't solve all the problems of knowing who said what either. Five of the letters of the Hebrew *alefbet* change form. Questions abound! Why these five letters? Which forms preceded which and which are more authoritative? Who decided? According to Rabbi Yirmeyah/Rabbi Ḥiyyah, the seers determined the form of the letters. But a seer is a threat to the authority of Reason. Having access to the Divine Intellect, such a person possesses great power, a dangerous and potentially destabilizing power that defies the stabilizing power of Reason. In fact, the gemara responds to this idea by bringing Rabbi Yirmeyah's/Rabbi Ḥiyya's statement into reasonable dialectic. It asks the question of Rabbi Yirmeyah's/Rabbi Ḥiyya's opening assertion in the text: "Is this reasonable"? It reminds us that the authoritative tradition has already ruled that prophets are not permitted to introduce anything new, basing this proposition on an interpretation of a statement in the Torah: "These are the commandments."

But, ironically, this interpretation is itself something new, something not explicitly found in the text. Thus, in challenging Rabbi Yirmeyah/Rabbi Ḥiyya, the gemara exercises a power that must masquerade as a prohibited power; that is, the power to innovate in the tradition through rational argumentation is challenged on the basis of reason. This challenge tames the seers, transforming them into the Prophets, authoritative spokesmen for the Divine. If even these authorized spokesmen are precluded from introducing anything new, how much more so the potentially renegade seers. They are interpreted out of existence, but their trace remains in the *sugya*.

To this Rabbi Ḥisda objects, despite the gemara's attempt to turn him into an ally. Rabbi Ḥisda tells us that the commandments were written to be seen from all sides! The same tablets could be read backward and forward, from one side or the other. And some of the letters could be held in place only miraculously. If someone hadn't come along and fixed the form of the letters of the Torah they might, even now, be floating in the air.

The gemara must concede: Yes, the letters of the Torah were fluid, requiring an effort of the Prophets (not seers) to bring them to a more reasonable order. Rabbi Ḥisda is mollified. But what about Reason? How can the gemara mollify Reason's claim that nothing new may be added to the Torah (even as Reason makes its claim through a new interpretation)? Only by asserting that what is new is never really new. It has only been forgotten and requires rediscovery. The Prophet and the exegete are, thus, in the same business—that of recovering lost knowledge. The letters miraculously stay in place until someone remembers how to read them.

The third reading of our passage thus uncovers a discussion of textuality and translation, the very subject and activity in which we are engaged. According to the gemara, there is a gap or opening between the original saying of a text and its written record. When we pass through this opening, we participate in a miracle. The letters are poised to float off the page but do not. Instead, their form, and ultimately their meaning, are fixed. The reader who can fix the form of the text must be someone committed to the tradition within which the text is read. But such a skilled reader is not free to jeopardize the society in which the text must function. A Prophet is needed, not a seer. At stake is the fundamental notion of the commandments, of our being commanded. The Prophet understands that the text functions not in some merely aesthetic mode, but as a bridge between each individual and his neighbor. The Prophet brings to his reading of the text (and prophets are readers of texts!) the cry of the oppressed and the command to respond to that cry. In so doing, of course, the Prophet is doing nothing new. He is only reminding us of our responsibilities. Establishing the text brings it, and us, back into existence, a world not limited by reason, but rather transcending reason by way of responsibility. The texts that facilitate such memory, thereby creating human beings, are in that way, divine.

3

THE PRACTICE OF TALMUD— THE READINGS

PRAYER AND THE END OF METAPHYSICS

Berakhot 8a

TEXT

"Therefore let every faithful man pray to You upon discovering [finding]." Rabbi Ḥanina says: "In the time of finding" refers to [the finding of] a wife. For it is said: Whoever finds a wife finds a great good. In the West [Palestine] they used to ask a man who married a wife thus: *matza* or *motze*? *Matza*, for it is written, "Whoever finds [*matza*] a wife finds a great good." *Motze*, for it is written, "And I find [*motze*] more bitter than death the woman." Rabbi Nathan says: "In the time of finding" refers to the [finding of] Torah. For it is said, "For whoever finds Me finds life," and so on. Rabbi Naḥman ben Isaac said: "In the time of finding" refers to [the finding of] death. For it is said, "The issues [*totza'ot*] of death." Similarly it has been taught: Nine hundred and three species of death were created in this world. For it is said: "The issues of death," and the numerical value of *totza'ot* is so. The worst of them is the croup, and the easiest of them is the kiss. Croup is like a thorn in a ball of wool pulled out backward. Some people say: It is like [pulling] a rope through the loopholes [of a ship]. [Death by a]

51

kiss is like drawing a hair out of milk. Rabbi Yoḥanan said: "In the time of finding" refers to the [finding of a] grave. Rabbi Ḥanina said: Which verse [may be quoted in support]? "Who rejoice unto exultation and are glad, when they can find the grave." Rabba son of Rabbi Shila said: Hence the proverb: A man should pray for peace even to the last clod of earth [thrown upon his grave]. Mar Zutra said: "In the time of finding," refers to the [finding of a] privy. They said in the West: This [interpretation] of Mar Zutra is the best of all.

INTERPRETATION

As we in the modern Western world become more sophisticated regarding matters of theology—or, more bluntly stated, as we lose faith—those of us seeking to conserve the habits of religious life seek for more and more sophisticated justifications for those habits, among them prayer. We seek to justify our engaging in activities in which we cannot simply believe. In part, our search emerges from our Western need for *system*, for logical consistency, for total consistency. This insistence on totality is a hallmark of all philosophic traditions stemming from the world of Greek philosophy (regardless of whether this accurately reflects that philosophy). This tradition culminates in the totalitarianism of scientific rationalism, popularly accepted as absolute truth in contemporary society. Our need for totality has forced those of us who would conserve religious living to justify that effort in terms that "make sense," not only in relation to outside systems but also within our own system. For example, we feel bound to pray to a God consistent with our study of philosophy, consistent with our mystical speculations, our political and moral initiatives, and any other mode of action and thought we engage in. Such need for consistency is a response to our yearning for intellectual totality, not a response to our own experience. Despite the ground gained over the past century by philosophies of experience, this more dominant trend has not slowed.

In this brief selection from Tractate *Berakhot*, you will find that we are not the first generation to consider this problem. The dangers of totalism were already recognized by the creators of the talmudic system that was in part created, I believe, to remain paradoxically unsystematic, an intellectually pluralistic system.

The central problem in our passage emerges from an exegesis of a verse from Psalm 32: "For this let everyone that is godly pray to You in the time of finding." In context, the simple meaning of the verse, though somewhat obscure, would seem to indicate that the devout ought to pray at a time when it is propitious for their prayers to be heard—that is, at a time when they might be "found" by God. Others have understood this verse as referring to the time that the devout person "finds" or discovers his sin. In either case, the psalmist might have meant: either at the appropriate times of public worship or at a time of intense private devotion. However, the rabbis in our passage understood this verse to refer not to the proper time for prayer but to the proper subject of prayer. "For this" one should pray, as opposed to "for" anything else. If we grant this understanding of the beginning of the verse, then we need to understand the end of the verse, which now becomes problematic. If we are praying for "a time of finding," then we must know what we are supposed to look for.

The question, "What is it proper to pray for?" is a question of theology, a question of systems. We have left the level of spontaneous religious act and have jumped to the level of philosophical reflection. Whether this leap itself is possible or justified will ultimately be taken up as part of our discussion. But we begin with the assumption that such a leap has taken place. Rabbi Ḥanina attempts to answer the question: What should we pray for? The answer: We pray for a good wife. The exegetical method of arriving at this answer, generally followed throughout this passage, need not long detain us. It is based on the occurrence of the same Hebrew root, *mem-tzadi-alef*, meaning "find," in different biblical contexts. In this first case, Rabbi Ḥanina suggests two occurrences of this root in reference to finding a wife. One is positive; the other is negative. He concludes that a man's happiness depends on finding a proper wife. Therefore, this is the most appropriate goal of prayer.

It is, of course, inconceivable that Rabbi Ḥanina believes that prayer should be restricted to men looking for wives. His statement and the text that includes it are not intended to be read literally. Rather, his statement must be understood theologically. What legitimate need and what justification for prayer can we extrapolate from Rabbi Ḥanina's example?

I would suggest that Rabbi Ḥanina's view refers generally to the blessings of material happiness. According to Rabbi Ḥanina, issues of family, work, health, and wealth are all acceptable subjects of prayer. For him, the leap from prayer to philosophic reflection on prayer is a short one. That which most people pray for is legitimate—with one caveat: One must pray only for that which is socially acceptable. Thus, to pray for an evil wife, and by extension, to pray for anything that is not materially beneficial, would not be permissible.

But Rabbi Nathan understands the psalmist differently. Using the same exegetical technique as Rabbi Ḥanina, he concludes that the "time of finding" refers not to material benefit but to Torah—that is, the proper goal of worship is knowledge. To pray for material needs is to attempt to manipulate the universe or the will of God. But to pray for Torah is to understand that the greatest act of Divine Providence is God's Revelation. To experience that revelation through Torah is the greatest good and the only legitimate focus of prayer. However, the particular verse in which Rabbi Nathan locates the root *mem-tzadi-alef* does not mention Torah. Rather, it speaks of finding *life*. Rabbi Nathan assumes that we understand that life is an analogue for Torah in the talmudic system, just as Torah is an analogue for life. Although Rabbi Nathan has leapt a little further than Rabbi Ḥanina in distancing our experience of prayer from its justification in satisfying our material desires, he still maintains the connection between prayer and life. According to him, we pray for Torah, for knowledge, which is, in fact, the primary "good" in this world. Prayer, for both Ḥanina and Nathan, is thus essentially utilitarian.

Rabbi Naḥman ben Isaac also struggles to understand the theological rationale for the act of prayer, but his understanding now takes us out of the world of the ordinary—literally, for he interprets the "time of finding" as a reference to death. Suddenly, our relationship to the exegesis in progress is shattered; the stakes in prayer are, at once, heightened and changed. Prayer is not to be understood as an act that can influence the worshiper's material life or spiritual/intellectual life. Rather, it is an act that focuses the worshiper's attention on the unavoidable confrontation with mortality. Simplistic notions of material or spiritual well-being are replaced by our consciousness of death. Everything palls in its presence.

Rabbi Naḥman's exegesis not only relies on the repetition of the root *mem-tzadi-alef*, but is also bolstered by the use of *gematria* (numerology) and traditional wisdom. We are thus told that "nine hundred and three species of death were created in this world. For it is said 'the issues *[toza'ot]* of death' and the numerical value of *toza'ot* is so." We should note that this leap from conceiving prayer as an act of simple religious faith to seeing it as a tool for metaphysical speculation about what life means in the face of death is accompanied by two sources of authority, one scriptural and the other extra-scriptural. We find this same pattern repeated in the next discussion about prayer that follows in the gemara. This "addition," so to speak, of a source of authority outside Scripture is neither accidental nor incidental. Just as we leave behind the *experience* of prayer as we reflect on it, so too we leave behind our relationship with Scripture as direct authority over our lives as we make room for human (that is, philosophical) sources of authority.

In the light of philosophy, the need for prayer in the face of mortality must be accounted for. The question is: What can the godly or pious reasonably pray for given that the purpose of prayer is to assist us in confronting our mortality? Should not philosophy, in fact, replace prayer in this confrontation? Do they not become synonymous? However, we learn that, because of the existence of easier and more difficult experiences of death, prayer can still have a legitimate role in a person's religious life, can still express a legitimate longing: That we experience an easy death rather than a difficult one.

The worst kind of death is the croup, described graphically as being like the experience of a thorn being pulled out of a ball of wool backward, shredding as it is pulled. Others say it is like experiencing the friction of a rope being pulled through the loopholes of a ship. The best kind of death is that which comes as a kiss, as gentle as drawing a hair out of milk.

The gemara reframes our question: What is a proper prayer for the pious, and at the same time addresses a deeper philosophic question: What is a proper prayer for those whose sophistication makes simple piety difficult? For the latter the subject has shifted. From a discussion about prayer we enter a discussion about death. While the pious person prays for an easy death, the philosophical person contemplates the meaning of the different kinds of death. A kiss, the easy death, requires an intimate. The croup is a cold, objective force. The one who pulls the rope or the thorn need not, cannot, truly be known to us. The one who kisses us must be known to us. A chasm opens beneath our feet. Will we be able to die as though we were bidding farewell to a loved one, or will we feel as though we were being torn apart? These are, on one level, certainly descriptions of the physical characteristics possible in various kinds of dying, but they also shed light on the nature of our relationships in the world. There are personalities implicit in this experience of death: Another person who is active in my experience of death and who comes to me either as a lover or as a stranger. The meaning of my death is inextricably tied to the quality of my relationship with this other person. It is a meaning that is captured in death but illuminates my life and is sought out in prayer, the experience itself now, which turns the stranger into the lover and thus defines my death and my life.

After all this, however, Rabbi Yoḥanan asserts that we have gone too far. The confrontation through prayer with mortality is not about ultimate meaning. Rather, it is about creating a social bond such that our death will be properly tended to. We cannot depend on creating a relationship of such intimacy that the sting of death will be removed. Yet, we can create enough of a presence in other people's lives to guarantee that our memory will be respected. This position is offered as another possible exegesis of the verse in Psalm 32 and is also supported by folk wisdom: "A man should pray for peace even to the last clod of earth thrown upon his grave." If the example of one's life cannot quell the inevitable squabbles between those he leaves behind at least long enough for them to bury him, his prayer-life has been insufficient.

So where does the Talmud leave us at the end of the discussion? Is the legitimate purpose of prayer to satisfy our material needs? To gain the wisdom of the spiritual life? To confront another person as lover rather than as stranger when we confront our mortality? Or to help us to lead our lives in such a way as to be worthy of respect and a peaceful end? To conclude our discussion, the gemara offers the exegesis of Mar Zutra, who states that a "time of finding" refers to the finding of a privy! Before we recover from our shock and dissolve into laughter, the gemara adds, in a relatively uncharacteristic conclusion, that they said in Palestine: "Mar Zutra's statement is the best of all!"

Humor intrudes/interrupts at two points in our passage—at the beginning and at the end. Both times it is introduced in the name of teachers from the "West." At the beginning of the passage comes some domestic humor in the form of a question "they" used to ask of a married man: *matza* or *motze*? Did you find a good wife or a woman more bitter than death? At the end the masters of the West are quoted again, ruling that Mar Zutra's outrageous assertion that finding a suitable place for a privy is the proper object of prayer. Sometimes, humor is the only legitimate philosophic stance. Sometimes, the rules of reflection and argumentation, the grandiose claims of philosophic speculation, so distort the immediacy of our experience as to render any philosophic stance ludicrous. At such times, the appropriate expression of philosophy's ludicrousness is a joke.

In its own circuitous way, the Talmud is teaching us that it is laughable to attempt to capture the meaning of prayer or its proper object philosophically. When trying to describe what to pray for, metaphysics runs into the absurd, for each person's experience of prayer is an experience that finally defies any reflection. Whether one prays for material or spiritual goods, whether one meditates on mortality or the shape of one's funeral, it is the same as praying for a privy when one needs it, or a beautiful day for a picnic or a good score on an exam. Praying is an act through which the individual aligns himself or herself with a complex axis—God, self, the other, and nature—that is larger than language and deeper than thought. Prayer humbles philosophy, teaching it to laugh at its own obsession with consistency, or to keep silent and stay out of the way.

TRANSLATION AND THE LIMITS OF LOGIC

Bava Metzia 20a–21a

TEXT

Mishnah

If one finds deeds of valuation, deeds of maintenance, documents of *halitzah* [rejection of levirate marriage] or refusal, documents of *berurin* (see below), or any other document issued by a court of law, one shall return them. If one finds [documents] in a small bag or in a case, [or if one finds] a roll or a bundle of documents, one shall return them. And how many documents constitute "a bundle"? Three fastened together. Rabban Simeon ben Gamaliel says: [If they belong to] one person who borrowed from three [lenders], one shall return them to the borrower; [if they belong to] three persons who borrowed from one [lender], one shall return them to the lender. If one finds a document among one's papers and does not know how it came there, it shall remain with him until Elijah comes. If notes of cancellation are found among them one must abide by the contents of the notes.

INTERPRETATION

The subject of this mishnah is the proper disposition of legal documents whose ownership is unclear. The concern of the mishnah was to insure that documents that effect a variety of legal changes, from changes in personal status to the transfer of property, were not lost before the actions they describe were properly completed. The return of the document to the wrong party could inadvertently bear witness to a legal act not yet properly accomplished; for instance, a note verifying that a debt had been repaid when it had not should certainly not fall into the hands of the debtor!

While the gemara follows the contours of this concern, it also introduces a subject quite apart from the concerns of the mishnah.

> What are documents of *berurin?*
> Here they translate: documents of claims.
> Rabbi Yirmeyah said: This one chooses one, and this one chooses one.

In this almost cryptically brief "dialogue" we find an introduction to the *sugya's* real subject: the problem of translation. The Gemara takes for granted that the word of God, as we human beings can experience it, is found in texts. These texts are divided between those that are called "written" and those that are called "oral." The written Torah is comprised of the Five Books of Moses and also includes all the books of the Hebrew Scriptures, the so-called "Old Testament." The oral Torah is comprised of the Mishnah and a collection of commentaries. Some of them, such as the Gemara, are commentaries on the Mishnah. Others are commentaries on the written Torah that go by the name Midrash. Among the latter, some are direct commentaries on the Holy Scripture—that is, they purport to tell us what those books say—whereas others are commentaries that attempt to ground the Mishnah in the written Scripture—that is, to eliminate any seeming contradiction between the two types of revelation.

The Gemara is acutely aware that the perception of God's word and God's will leads through a labyrinth of texts, each of which requires explanation. Since the Bible and the Mishnah are written in Hebrew, whereas the rest of the oral Torah is primarily in Aramaic, at the least, they require translation and then explanation. Our *sugya* tackles this problem head-on. The opening sentences lay out the problem clearly. First, the question: "What are documents of *berurin?*" The question is a twofold one: "How do we translate the word *berurin* into Aramaic?" and "What are the legal implications of the mishnah's laws governing the finding of documents of *berurin?*" We deduce the first question from the answer: "Here they translate: documents of claims." The use of the word *tergamu*, "they translate," is not accidental. There are other satisfactory ways in which the gemara could have said either "they explained," or "they said," or "they taught," but the gemara is asking about the meaning of the Hebrew word *berurin*. It is also interested in the legal application of the word. With consummate economy, this single statement answers both questions simultaneously: "deeds of argument." These documents, deeds that set forth the claims of one party against another, must be returned to the prosecuting party if found. The gemara understands that it is these documents that the mishnah meant to include in its use of this word. However, Rabbi Yirmeyah, a rabbi from the land of Israel, informs us that *shitrei berurin* meant something quite different in Palestine: documents in which parties to a dispute list their choices for arbitrators. The gemara records Rabbi Yirmeyah's statement without further comment. Why?

Knowing the literal meaning of words in one language is not the same thing as being able to translate them into another language. The problem of translation is to achieve not only faithfulness to the literal meaning, but also faithfulness to all that is conveyed by a word in its original language. As the translated word is placed into its new linguistic, cultural, and legal context, it offers an opportunity for interpretation, and sometimes even provides the rationale for rabbinic legislation. That the gemara sticks with its translation of *shitrei berurin* in the face of Rabbi Yirmeyah's literal translation, that it does not even comment on his statement and certainly does not try to deny it, further emboldens us to suggest that the literal meaning of a phrase is precisely *not* its translation—that a word or phrase *gains* meaning in translation.

The problems of translation take on greater significance when we are dealing with the words of God. Whether we call these words religious or mythic, whether or not we know for certain that the authors of the gemara believed them to be divine, the fact that they called the Mishnah *oral* Torah cannot be overlooked. Though we are dealing with the details of commercial transactions, a subject that does not impress us as being particularly "religious," the Gemara is always operating in the context of explicating the word of God as revealed in and through the Mishnah. That translation is the only way one can begin to understand the word of God.

The gemara now proceeds to explore the legal problem in more detail. Beginning with the next phrase in the mishnah, the gemara continues its discussion.

> "And all court-related documents, he should return." That bill of divorce that was found in Rabbi Ḥuna's courtroom, in which it was written: "In the city of Sheviri, on the Rakhis River." Rabbi Ḥuna said: We are concerned about two Sheviris. Rabbi Ḥisda said to Rabba: "Go out and consider for this evening, for Rabbi Ḥuna will ask you about it." He went out, examined the matter and found. For we have learned: "Any decision of a court shall be returned."

The gemara cites an incident in the court of Rabbi Ḥuna in which a bill of divorce was found. Before considering it effective, Rabbi Ḥuna raises some concerns as to our ability to know for whom it was written. Rabbi Ḥisda suggests that Rabba investigate the matter and be prepared to report later that evening. He does so, and, on the basis of our mishnah, suggests the ruling that the divorce be considered as completed because we have learned: "Any decision of a court shall be returned."

We tend to approach the Gemara with the solemnity we believe due a sacred text. While this is generally appropriate, it can obscure the fact that the Gemara is often quite funny. Humor can be necessary, when we tread on sacred ground, to help us maintain our humility. There can be little doubt that this story concerning the court of Rabbi Ḥuna is humorous. The very fact that Rabba is sent to "find" something and returns having "found" it alerts us to the plots within plots that this *sugya* presupposes. We are discussing lost objects and Rabba is out finding texts. The text he finds is the very one that we, the audience, are reading. Did Rabbi Ḥuna not know about this mishnah? When Rabbi Amram challenges Rabba's "find" is he challenging only the logic, or is he also suggesting that the "find" itself is laughable, given that it explicates a text with the very text we are trying to explicate?

The conclusion also attests to some self-deprecating humor in this discussion, for the very walls of the academy crack in response to the debate that ensues.

> Rabbi Amram said to Rabba: "How can you, sir, derive a ritual law from monetary matters?" He said to him: "Fool! We have learned "deeds of *halitzah* or *meyun!*" The cedar column supporting the study-house cracked. One said: It cracked because of my luck, and the other said: it cracked because of my luck.

Rabbi Amram challenges Rabba about a matter that seems explicit in the mishnah—that is, although the mishnah is dealing with matters that are essentially "monetary" (in that they affect the property of individuals involved), the mishnah's examples include matters from the category of ritual law rather than business law. Rabbi Amram's objection to Rabba's deriving a ritual law from a business law is also an objection to the mishnah's similar combination of the two, for Rabba is only following the mishnah, whereas Rabbi Amram is, apparently, reading the mishnah differently. The difference is important. Consider this list in the mishnah:

> If one found letters of assessment, or letters of maintenance, deeds of *ḥalitzah*, or *meyun*, or deeds of *berurin*, or any court decision, he should return them.

For Rabba all of its subjects are equal—that is, "or any court decision" is an equal part of the list. Rabbi Amram, on the other hand, appears to read the mishnah's list to mean that *these documents* and only these documents should be returned, including deeds of *berurin*. Otherwise, each of these documents might not be included in the more general category that follows: "all court decisions should be returned." We have moved from the question of the meaning of the words of the mishnah to the question of the grammar of the mishnah, the ways in which a simple list can be read.

We should not be surprised by this move. Lists are an important genre in biblical literature, as well as in rabbinic literature. Genealogies, lists of materials, and lists of prohibited and permitted foods, marriages, and a variety of other items abound. Rabbinic literature devotes considerable energy to determining the proper way of reading such lists in the Bible and in the Mishnah. The question of determining and distinguishing between general propositions and particular propositions, and between inclusive and exclusive statements, is a central element of the interpretive process. Although we do not have a full-blown discussion of these issues in our *sugya*, their presence should not be overlooked.

If we hoped for a definitive answer to this question of reading lists, the conclusion of the story disappoints. We are left not with rational argumentation but with the seeming intercession of the divine directly into the debate, in a way that only the divine can intercede: the columns of the academy house crack. No one could ask for a more direct sign from God, if only we knew on whose side God was! Not unexpectedly, each of the disputants claims this divine intercession on his behalf. The gemara does not choose between them, and we are left, once again, to wonder: how do we decipher the will of God? If through direct experience, how do we translate that experience such that it makes sense? And if through texts, how do we read *and* translate those texts such that we can apply them? Simply following the text, as Rabba does, will, apparently, not do.

Thus we are forced to forge ahead in our study of the mishnah with these questions still in mind.

> "If he found them in a *hafisa.*" What is a *hafisa?* Rabba bar Bar Hana said: A small leather bag. What is *d'luskama?* Rabba bar Samuel said: A case carried by old people.

As the gemara proceeds, it confronts yet again the problem of understanding the terms used in the mishnah, the Hebrew word *hafisa* and the Greek word *d'luskama.* Up to now, we have accepted the premise that the Hebrew of the mishnah might be occasionally difficult to translate. Here it is as hard to translate as is the Greek. It is difficult not to apply the phrase, "It was Greek to me," to the discussion! In both cases, the translations are made quickly so as to introduce the more complex problem of translating the concepts they represent. As the subject of translation is broadened to include the act of interpretation itself, translation and interpretation become two sides of the same coin.

The gemara continues:

> "A roll of documents or a bundle of documents." Our Rabbis taught: "How many are a 'roll of documents'? Three rolled together. And how many are a 'bundle of documents'? Three tied together."

Even when we know the simple meaning of the words of the mishnah, the work of translation is not finished. It continues under the guise, if you will, of interpretation. As soon as the interpretive problem has been stated, the application of logic is begun. Further, the application of logic includes and perhaps requires argumentation. In the gemara's words:

> You may infer from this: A knot is an identification mark. But surely Rabbi Hiyya taught: "Three rolled together"! If so, this is a roll!

That is to say, according to our definition of a bundle they are tied together. If so, it is logical to ask the owner to identify such a bundle by its knot. This is, however, objected to on the basis of a teaching by Rabbi Hiyya that describes a bundle as being three rolled together, not tied, and without a knot. But if we accept this teaching of Rabbi Ḥiyya, then the distinction we have made between a bundle and a roll is no longer valid. Rabbi Ḥiyya's bundle is the same as our roll. The process of argumentation forces us to hone our reasoning more finely. We devise a new interpretation/translation. In the case of a bundle the documents lie flat, one on top of the other. In the case of a roll the pages are intertwined such that the beginning of one document is folded into the next document.

Logic has not failed us, but neither has it answered all of our questions as yet. For the gemara continues:

> What does [the finder] announce? The number. [Then] why does [the mishnah] speak of three? Even two also. Rather, as Rabina said:[The finder] announces "coins." Here too, [the finder] announces: "Documents."

As a consequence of our deduction that there is no knot on a bundle or a roll by which it can be identified, the gemara is interested in understanding exactly what the finder should announce in order to entice a person looking for something to investigate what has been found. It suggests that the finder should announce the number of documents that have been found. But if that were so, then why would the mishnah have stipulated, as part of its definition of both a bundle and a roll, that they are made up of three documents? Why not two? Thus, the number of documents cannot be the identifying principle. Instead, we follow the ruling of Rabina who said that in the case of found coins the finder announces, "coins," and similarly in the case of documents one should announce, "documents."

Our dependence on reason for the ongoing translation/interpretation of the mishnah appears to be wholly sufficient for our purposes. However, as the gemara begins to ask more complex questions concerning the very nature of the documents we have found, we find that matters are not so simple. Even when we understand the surface meaning of the words, and when we have answered the obvious logistical questions, questions about what we can actually know about documents, their meaning and the intent of their authors become far more troubling. We begin to move into the heart of this discussion: What can one truly know about the meaning of a document? And especially: How much by logic?

The gemara goes on to explicate three sentences in the mishnah. The first two of the explications take the following pattern. A sentence is quoted from the mishnah, then an assertion is made by the gemara that a contrary ruling by the mishnah would have made no sense—that is, no logical sense. This, in turn, is challenged by finding life situations that might show that a contrary ruling *would* have been possible in life in what we might call common sense, rather than strict logic. This, in turn, is denied, not by the application of logic, but by common sense itself, proving that logic and common sense, reason and real life, agree.

The third explication follows a similar pattern, but the differences are suggestive. First of all, only one part of the sentence is explicated. Another is skipped over silently. Second, this explication begins by modifying the case in the mishnah by the addition of another named source. Because of these similarities and the suggestive nature of the differences, we will consider these three units together.

> "Rabban Simeon ben Gamaliel says: One [borrower] who borrowed from three [lenders, the finder] should return [the documents] to the borrowers, and so on." For if you were to imagine that [the documents] are the lenders', what are they doing together? Perhaps they went to certify them? Here they had already been certified. Perhaps they fell from the scribe's hand? A person does not leave his certified [document] in the scribe's hands.

> "Three who borrowed from one [the finder] should return [the document], and so on." For, if you were to imagine that they are the borrower's, what are they doing together? Perhaps they went [to the same scribe] to write them? Here [the documents] were written in three hands. But perhaps they went to certify them? The lender certifies his note; the debtor does not certify his document.

> "If there are notes of cancellation among them, he should do what is in the notes of cancellation." Rabbi Yirmeyah bar Abba said in the name of Rav: "A note of cancellation that is found in the possession of the lender, even though it is written in his handwriting, is nothing but a trick and is invalid. There is no need to state this when it is written in a scribe's hand, where it is possible to say that the scribe happened [to be there] and wrote it, but even where it was written in [the lender's] own hand, it is invalid. [For the lender] thinks: 'Perhaps [the borrower] will come by chance [on Friday] at dusk, and pay me. For, if I do not give him [a note of cancellation], he will not give me the money; [so] I will write [the receipt now], so that when he brings me the money, I will give him [the note].'"

> We have learned [in the mishnah]: "If there are notes of cancel-
> lation among them, he should do what is in the notes of cancella-
> tion"! As Rabbi Safra said: Where it was found among torn notes.
> Here, too, where he found it among torn notes.

The language of the first two units in this triad is straightforward, and
the law is not affected. The rulings of the mishnah are affirmed: documents must be returned. What, then, is the literary or philosophical
force of performing these quasi-analyses on the language of the mishnah? Perhaps to show that when reason is applied to the text to justify
its conclusion, we simply end by affirming the common practice of people. Whether we continue to assume that our question is "How do we
read texts?" or "How do we translate texts?" the conclusion would
seem to be that we read or translate texts on the basis of the common-
sense activities of ordinary people in an everyday context.

The third unit in our triad, then, can be read as exploring a further
challenge to this conclusion. It attempts to prove that there must be
something more reliable than everyday life to aid us in translating the
word of God. It begins by attempting to understand the mishnah in
terms of another unit of rabbinic teaching. The particular unit it
chooses, however, is one that contains within it a less than subtle reminder of just how unreliable documents can be. For, we learn in the
statement of Rabbi Yirmeyah bar Abba in the name of Rav that a note of
cancellation written by a lender and, by implication, found in a lender's
possession, is to be considered nothing or a joke. Thus, the ruling of our
mishnah is challenged, and the notion that we can determine the meaning of documents is also challenged. In this case, again, common sense
is brought to bear on the situation, and an everyday setting is found in
which the action of this lender is understood to be other than a trick.
However, this example does not suffice, for the gemara now uses the
teaching of the mishnah itself—the sentence we are studying ("If notes
of cancellation are found among them, one must abide by the contents
of the notes")—to challenge the need for such a reconstruction of everyday life. The law ought to be perfectly clear on its own. If it is, then the
problem becomes a new one—that is: How can we harmonize two con-
flicting rabbinic teachings, that of the mishnah and that of Rabbi
Yirmeyah bar Abba in the name of Rav? This harmonization is accomplished through a third teaching, that of Rabbi Safra, who stated that
the note in question was found among torn documents—that is, documents whose legal matters had been effected. Therefore, this note, too,
should be considered as one that had been effected. This third teaching

re-establishes the primacy of common sense and common practice as the arbiter of a text's meaning. This would appear to be the conclusion of this three-part unit and a tentative answer to the larger question we are asking. We translate texts—that is, understand the word of God—on the basis of human institutions and custom.

This is not the gemara's final word on the matter in our *sugya*. Before following *that* discussion, however, we must account for a discussion that is not here. Keeping in mind that the makers of the gemara were acutely sensitive to texts and that they, like us, had the mishnah literally before their eyes, we must ask why the following sentence from the mishnah, ostensibly belonging to the group of sentences we have just examined, is not included in the discussion. Its absence is felt and should not be considered accidental. It is: "If one found a document among one's documents and does not know what its nature is, it should remain [with him] until Elijah comes."

On the level of law this statement is not problematic. After all, our entire discussion is aimed precisely at discovering what the nature of a particular document is. If we cannot do so, then we have no choice but to await the end of time to discover its true owner. Why, then, is this line ignored? Lines that are passed over silently have a strange way of speaking out all the more loudly. This line in the mishnah is, in fact, the most problematic of all from the perspective of our larger questions concerning the nature of texts and the nature of the word of God. Are we left with no recourse but awaiting the proverbial forerunner of the Messiah when confronted by texts (or experiences) whose nature we cannot immediately determine? This line in the mishnah challenges the very enterprise on which the gemara is founded. Yet, up to this point in the discussion, we have established only that our alternative to "waiting" is relying on local custom. The concluding segments of the gemara must be read in light of the tension between these two possibilities.

This tension is explored in a series of four subunits of text, each beginning with the phrase, "Come and hear." Following these subunits, we reach the final discussion of this *sugya* in which the tension will be resolved. The introductory phrase "come and hear" is generally used to alert us to an objection being brought to a particular argument from the oral Torah tradition, either from the Mishnah itself or from a *baraita,* a teaching in the name of one of the mishnaic masters that is not found in the codified Mishnah. It is not unreasonable to conclude that, in our case, at least, this barrage of quotations from the oral Torah tradition against Rabbi Safra's position (that is, that the mishnah is applicable only within the bounds of local custom and common sense, that neither pure logic nor adherence to tradition will suffice) is as much a part of the structure of this discussion as is the determination of the particular law.

> Come and hear: "[If a note] is found [by a lender] among his documents [stating that] Josef ben Simeon's promissory note has been repaid, both of their promissory notes are [considered to have been] repaid"!
>
> As Rabbi Safra said: Where it was found among torn notes. Here, too, where it was found among torn notes.
>
> Come and hear: "[We declare on] oath that father did not instruct us, and that father did not tell us, and that we did not find [a note] among father's documents [stating] that this [promissory] note was repaid."
>
> Rabbi Safra said: Where it was found among torn notes.
>
> Come and hear: "A note of cancellation that has [the signatures of] witnesses on it should be authenticated by the signatures on it."
>
> Say: It should be authenticated by those who signed it. For we ask the witnesses if it has been repaid [or] if it has not been repaid.
>
> Come and hear: "A note of cancellation that has witnesses on it is valid." What are "witnesses"? Witnesses [that it was] certified.
>
> Indeed, this stands to reason, for the last clause teaches: "But [one] that has no witnesses on it is invalid." What is "one that has no witnesses on it"? If you say that there are no witnesses on it at all, is it necessary to say that it is invalid? Rather, is it not [referring to] witnesses [that it was] certified?

In each "come and hear" statement, a mishnah or *baraita* is used to support the position of the mishnah without the aid of local custom. In each of the first two cases, however, Rabbi Safra's statement is required in order for the law not to violate such custom. In the third, this approach is abandoned or modified. Instead of relying on local custom, we take up the subject of attestation. What is the effect of witnesses on the validity of a document? If witnesses cannot be believed, how could any document be taken seriously? In fact, we learn that all documents, by their very nature as documents, are assumed to have witnesses. That additional step is what makes them documents. However, there is a kind of attestation that goes beyond the formation of a document and requires a special understanding of the nature of witnesses. That is certification, or the attestation by a third party that either the witnesses or whatever other circumstances are being used to validate the document are themselves valid. And certification is the category in which a document is transformed from a passive to an active instrument. Therefore, the requirements for what attests to certification become the subject of our final unit of discussion and the final word of this *sugya* on the problem of reading and translating texts.

> Returning to the subject [literally, "the thing itself"]: "A note of cancellation that has [the signatures of] witnesses on it should be authenticated by the signatures on it. One that does not have [the signatures of] witnesses on it and is produced by a third party, or one that appears below the document's signatures, is valid." "One that is produced by a third party" [is valid], because the lender trusted the third party. "One that appears below the document's signatures"[is valid] too, because if [the debt] had not been repaid, [the lender] would not have invalidated his [own promissory] note.

From the beginning of our *sugya*, several actors have lurked in the background: the writer of a document, the intended audience of a document, and the finder of a document. The first two actors have been silent. We do not have their evidence at all. The finder of the document has been the active player, and his relationship as a third party to the original events has been the chief item of concern. Being a third party to a document, to an agreement, is a role that the finder discovers is problematic. In attempting to clarify this role, the gemara appeals to that institution of being a third party that is natural to documents: witnesses. The gemara says that it is witnesses who bring a document into existence. Without them, the document has no life. It is to the witnesses, the original witnesses and the witnesses of certification, that we must turn in order to determine the status of a document.

In doing this, the gemara turns to "the thing itself." This phrase is used often to focus a discussion in the gemara on a particular text that was itself brought into the discussion in order to make a particular point, not in order to become the focus of explication. With the term *gufa*, the gemara treats the particular text in the same way it would treat any other unit of text: as a whole. In this case, the particular text establishes a functional equality between a witness to a document and a third party who has been given possession of a document, as well as a functional equality between either of these two and a document written under or after the signatures. In this case, at least, "the thing itself" indicates the gemara's turn to address the major underlying question of the *sugya*.

A document in a commercial transaction can be presumed to be valid if it either has valid witnesses, is in the possession of an appointed third party, or is written beneath the signatures of the parties. These facts settle the surface legal discussion, even as they deepen immeasurably the larger philosophical discussion. We return again to our notion that the subject beneath the subject of our *sugya* is translation and, specifically, the translation of the word of God in experience and in text. Our discussion posits that the very existence of a document is dependent on witnesses. Who are the witnesses to the Torah tradition, oral and written? If the parties to the document are God and Israel, who can serve as witness? In the Torah itself, God calls upon heaven and earth to witness the transactions between God and Israel. But the heavens and earth are mute. To whom, then, do we turn? To a third party, the outsider, the other. It is s/he who validates the agreement between God and Israel. It is the third party, trusted by at least one party of the agreement, who validates it. In lieu of the third party, able to act, as it were, in his stead, is a document written beneath or after the signatures. These are the two, as yet cryptic, solutions to the problem at hand. The translation of God's originally witnessed word is through its re-creation into a document validated by third parties, or by the writing of documents below the signatures. How do we unpack this cryptic solution?

It is less complicated than it might at first appear. Speaking out of its contemporary niche, but speaking authentically for us today, the gemara suggests two distinct, though not necessarily antithetical, modes to validate a translated document. The original document, the Torah, is witnessed but the witnesses are mute. As we go about the business of translating and validating Torah, we must look to the third party, the one who is not party to the original agreement, for validation. Who is this other? There might be those who would see in that role later generations of Jews, the guardians, as it were, of the original agreement. I am not inclined to this approach. The gemara will offer a second role, that of textual continuity, as the specifically Jewish stake in the process of translation and validation. Furthermore, difficult as it is to maintain in the face of a bloody history, the Torah purports to be an agreement with the People of Israel on behalf of humanity. If the Torah is the agreement binding Israel to God, then the final arbiter of the effectiveness of that agreement is not the Jewish people itself, but all of humanity. Therefore, the other in our *sugya* is just that: those who are not party to the original agreement. Jewish society—that is, Torah—is judged by the righteousness of those who are not Jewish. The validation of the Torah is in the hands of those who will judge whether the life of the Torah's devotee bespeaks a divine text. Not local custom, not our institutions, not logic, but righteousness as perceived by the outsider determines the validity of the word of God.

But not only that. The third party calls us to righteousness. So do the signatures at the top of the document. The gemara's tradition of interpretation continues, as it were, the writing of the document beneath the signatures. The signatures may be of the parties themselves, God and Israel. They may be of the witnesses, the heavens and earth, the natural world, in which Israel's mandate to pursue the divine mandate is discovered. They may be all of these and more. What is most crucial is that the documents that come later are validated by the testimony of all that came before. Translating the word of God accurately ultimately depends on either the validation of the stranger, the third party, and/or the faithful continuity of the tradition itself. The effort to translate and interpret provides the role for a specifically Jewish validation of the document, but its implications in the life of the world stand as its ultimate validation.

THE SEARCH FOR MEANING AND THE MEANING OF THE SEARCH

Pesaḥim 7b–8a

TEXT

Our Rabbis taught: One may not search either by the light of the sun, or by the light of the moon, or by the light of a torch, save by the light of a lamp, because the light of a lamp is suitable for searching. And though there is no proof of the matter yet there is a memory of this thing, for it is said, "No leaven shall be found in your houses for seven days" (Exod. 12:19), and it is said, "He searched, beginning with the oldest" (Gen. 44:12), and it is said, "At that time, I will search Jerusalem with lamps" (Zeph. 1:12), and it is said, "The lifebreath of man is the lamp of the LORD, revealing all his inmost parts" (Prov. 20:27).

This light of the sun, where is it meant? Shall we say, in a courtyard? But Raba said: A courtyard does not require searching, because birds frequent it. While if in a hall . . . But Raba said: A hall is searched by its own light? This is meant only in respect of a skylight in a room. But [then] what part of it? If [that which is] opposite the skylight, then it is the same as a hall? Rather, it means [the part of the room] at the sides.

And not [by the light of] a torch? Surely Raba said, What is the meaning of the verse: "It is a brilliant light/Which gives off rays on every side—/And therein His glory is enveloped" (Hab. 3:4). To what are the righteous comparable in the presence of the Shekhinah? To a lamp in the presence of a torch. And Raba also said: [To use] a torch for *havdalah* is the most preferable [way of performing this] duty? Said Rabbi Naḥman ben Isaac: The one can be brought into holes and cracks [in the wall], whereas the other cannot be brought into holes and chinks. Rabbi Zebid said: The one [throws] its light forward whereas the other [throws] its light behind. Rabbi Papa said: Here [with a torch] one is afraid, whereas there [with a lamp] one is not afraid. Rabina said: The light of the one is steady, whereas that of the other is fitful.

INTERPRETATION

I

The practice of *bedikat ḥametz*, the search for leaven, is, and always was, largely symbolic. One certainly cannot wait until the night before Pesaḥ to begin looking for *ḥametz*. The search is the conclusion of our eliminating *ḥametz*, something of a statement of preparedness for Pesaḥ. However, on a deeper level, *bedikat ḥametz* suggests itself as a symbol for a spiritual process. It is an elaborate ritual that dramatizes the necessary inner preparations Pesaḥ requires. It is, I am convinced, in this spirit that this rabbinic discussion should be understood.

The Talmud is interested in two broad questions:

1. What is leaven? That is, what does the symbol of leaven stand for?
2. How is it exposed and extirpated?

The attempt to answer the first question begins by working through an answer to the second. Leaven, the kind of spiritual leaven we are interested in, is that which is hidden. It cannot be seen in the light of day, nor of night. It cannot be seen even in the bright artificial light of a torch. It is hidden in such a way as to preclude discovery in the noise and distraction of everyday affairs. It requires the quiet, fragile, and private light symbolized by a small lamp or candle. The question of this light and its nature will occupy us later in the discussion. First, we need to investigate more closely the nature of that which is hidden and the nature of our search for it.

The Talmud tells us that learning about the nature of this hiddenness is not something that can be ascertained by logical proof. Rather, it will be discovered by virtue of a historical memory: "There is no proof, but a memory of this thing." Now, it should be noted that the phrase *zekher le-devar* is usually translated as "a hint of the matter." But this translation is misleading. There is a more common Hebrew word for hint, *remez*, which is used also in Aramaic. The choice here of the word *zekher*, memory, should not be treated lightly. In fact, in order to discover something about our search we need to enter the source for all Jewish memory, the Torah. The memories of the searches we will encounter in the Torah, memories that all Jews are expected to have in an almost genetic way, teach us some very important lessons regarding the environment in which our search ought to take place.

First of all, the requirement itself to search comes from the Torah: "No leaven shall be found in your houses for seven days"(Exod. 12:9). This is actually a requirement not to search for but to find. We know that it implies a search from analogy with another historic memory, a verse in Genesis that uses the same word, "found," regarding the search by Joseph's servants of his brothers' belongings. In the course of this search they find the money and silver goblet that Joseph has planted in Benjamin's sack.

Is this not an unusual historic memory to stir up before Pesaḥ: The terrible conflict between Joseph and his brothers? The near murder of Joseph at his brothers' hands on account of his pride and arrogance and their jealousy? Joseph's enslavement and subsequent rise to power over them? His punishment of his brothers through his attacks on Benjamin? The brothers' ultimate loyalty to Jacob and Benjamin, the reversal of character from the days of Joseph's youth that leads to their weeping at his feet and, in turn, leads Joseph to reveal himself and be reconciled to them? What does this story have to do with leaven? Perhaps everything. Clearly, the Rabbis read the story of Joseph and his brothers as a prefigurement of the story of Israel in Egypt—a double prefigurement, if you will. The story itself—the envy and anger between brothers, leading to slavery; the pain and punishment of the perpetrators, leading to revelation and reconciliation—provides us with a "memory" of what we are looking for when we search for *ḥametz*. We are looking for just that pride, envy, and unconcern for our sibling (Joseph) and our parent (Jacob)—all people are to be considered as our siblings and all traditional wisdom, as our parents—that have led and will lead inevitably to slavery and death.

The second prefigurement of the story is, of course, literal. After all, it was through Joseph that the Jewish people came to be in Egypt, a fact that itself raises questions for further reflection. Joseph's sojourn in Egypt saved the Jewish people physically. Famine was conquered, but, one might conclude, this physical salvation, when unaccompanied by a spiritual component, results only in slavery. All of this is a *zekher*—a memory—that we bring to the search for leaven.

Having established this memory of what we are searching for, the *baraita* builds its next level in order to answer its question: By what light do we search? This time our memory comes from the prophet Zephaniah. We must always consider the context of all biblical verses quoted by the Rabbis very seriously. The Rabbis were well aware of the contexts out of which they quoted and expected that their readers also would be. Simply to interpret individual verses as if they had no context is methodologically unsound.

The search, established by our first biblical quotation as having a connection somewhat indirectly with pride, envy, and unconcern, is now more directly identified. The candle/lamp is now the instrument of a divine search. And the search is for the kind of evil for which, the prophet informs us, God is prepared to destroy the world. Specifically, a time of judgment is at hand: God, we are told, is preparing a feast (perhaps a Pesaḥ?). God bids the guests purify themselves and announces that, before the feast, God will search Jerusalem with a lamp/candle. "And I will punish the men/ Who rest untroubled on their lees,/ Who say to themselves,/ 'The LORD will do nothing, good or bad'" (Zeph. 1:12).

We now have a clearer picture of the historic memory we are trying to recover in order to understand the symbol of *bedikat ḥametz*. We are searching for pride, envy, and unconcern for others, coupled with an arrogant dismissal of God's justice. And we are searching for it with a lamp/candle similar to that used by God. To investigate the nature of this light a little more, our historical memory is directed to another source, one from Proverbs. Once again, the context of the verse is the conclusion of a litany of Israel's offenses, a list of moral failures to which we are prone. "Bread gained by fraud may be tasty to a man,/ But later his mouth will be filled with gravel./ . . . One who reviles his father or mother,/ Light will fail him when darkness comes . . . " (Prov. 20:17, 20). Claiming that moral decision-making is the central source of human meaning, the text enjoins: "A wise king winnows out the wicked,/ And turns the wheel upon them./ The lifebreath of man is the lamp of the LORD/ Revealing all his inmost parts" (Prov. 20:26–27). The light we must use to find and extirpate our moral failures, the light that has been used historically to search out the soul of Israel, finds her inevitable failures and guides her from slavery to redemption by way of reconciliation. This is the light of God within us. *Bedikat ḥametz* is intended to force us, through the power of ritual, to discover the light of God within us and to turn it on those character traits that inevitably lead to slavery, so that we can purify ourselves before the "sacrificial meal" of God and find redemption.

II

A relatively short discussion of this *baraita* by the *Amoraim* follows. It is couched in the language of halakhah—prescriptive law. But we must keep in mind that the law is never seriously in question. Rather, the discussion seems to plumb the law's reasoning but takes the law itself for granted. Philosophical or theological principles are raised tangentially, in an unfocused manner. Although a discussion of these methods of discourse is not germane to our present purpose, it undergirds all that I am claiming. Indeed, the philosophical or theological issues masked by the formal discussion of legal minutiae represent the unstated but unmistakable purpose of the text.

The gemara asks: What does the *baraita* mean by excluding the light of the sun as a source by which to search for *ḥametz*? It explains that the only place in which the sun would be good for searching would be an outdoor courtyard, but Raba has already taught: "A courtyard does not require searching because birds frequent it"—that is, birds would have eaten any crumbs dropped there. Can we then deduce from this principle that that part of our lives exposed to broad daylight is not the part we have to search because exposure to public criticism "keeps us clean"? The Rabbis might very well intend such a deduction.

The gemara then asks: What about searching in a hall—that is, a kind of porch or piazza, open on top but formed by pillars? But Raba contends that "a hall is searched by its own light." Commentators recognize a problem here: If the hall is searched by its own light because it is open on top, why can't the same be said of a courtyard? If so, we would apply to it the previous ruling. And if it is not an open courtyard, then what is it? Why is it searched by its own light, in contradistinction to the general ruling of our mishnah? Commentators and the general sense of the gemara agree: Raba could not have thought that the hall was a courtyard but rather was thinking of an indoor, covered hallway with its own skylight. Although natural light may indeed be sufficient to search the public space, Raba claims that the candle/lamp is still necessary for "the sides"—that is, the places not exposed to public scrutiny, the private places, the innards, the heart. Raba's explanation of our *baraita* only supports our previous understanding of it.

And now we come to the final parry, the final Torah verse, the final sacred memory of our passage. The gemara asks: "And not by the light of a torch?"—that is, the light of a torch cannot be used; why? This question is even more pressing once we see that regarding a torch the gemara can even cite a teaching by Raba himself that would seem to indicate that a torch is *preferable* to a candle/lamp. Such a teaching would undo our understanding of the verses previously cited by the *baraita*, as well as threaten the law. For Raba teaches: [What is the meaning of the verse?] "It is a brilliant light/ Which gives off rays on every side—/ And therein his glory is enveloped" (Hab. 3:4)? To what are the righteous compared in the presence of the *Shekhinah?* To a lamp in the presence of a torch. Even Raba agrees that a torch, comparable to the light of God, is more powerful than a lamp/candle, comparable to humans in the presence of God. Further, says Raba, "It is preferable to use a torch for *havdalah,*" thus implying that a torch is preferable to a lamp for the performance of mitzvot since we already know that torches are used to fulfill a religious obligation during the ceremony ending the Sabbath.

Before we see how the gemara responds to this serious thrust, we must tread all the pathways of this argument. What may appear to us merely as an argument may well mask a new level of theological speculation, for, here, the gemara manages to introduce a new biblical text—and a fascinating interpretation of that text—having to do with the subject of light, one of our two original subjects. It also introduces another occasion on which light is used, the end of Shabbat. Light is a theme of Shabbat as well as one of our themes.

What is light? It is the extension of God into the world. A larger quotation from the prophet Habakkuk, the source quoted by Raba, makes this clear:

God is coming from Teman,
The Holy One from Mount Paran.
His majesty covers the skies,

His splendor fills the earth:
It is a brilliant light
Which gives forth rays on every side—
And therein His glory is enveloped.
Pestilence marches before Him,
And plague comes forth at His heels.

(Hab. 3:3–5)

All of our themes are contained in these remarkable verses! God is light. The righteous, according to Raba, are the rays that come forth from His hand. His power is hidden (and must be found?!) and before it can be found, pestilence and plague must be endured; His justice must be served. Though used by the gemara seemingly to oppose our interpretation, these verses, in fact, are the most striking example yet of the themes we have tried to explicate: of God as the source of light and of something less than God's light (a candle/lamp) existing within us—the spark of our righteousness.

Finally, the text refers to the ceremony of *havdalah*. At the close of Shabbat, we separate from redemption, sadly recognizing that once again it has not yet occurred. The light of the torch represents/symbolizes the light of God, the God of redemption. The torch represents God's presence in a redeemed world, not in a world characterized by pride, envy, and a lack of compassion. In our as-yet-unredeemed world, God has been reduced to a candle or a lamp—a spark of righteousness—with which—or by whose light—we must search our inner life and rid it of that which stands between us and redemption.

Beginning with Rabbi Naḥman, the text gives four straightforward rationalizations for our needing to use a candle or lamp rather than a torch when searching for *ḥametz*, and each argument is equally relevant to the symbolic-philosophic themes we have been developing. First, Rabbi Naḥman ben Isaac explains: "The one [a candle/lamp] can be brought into holes and cracks, whereas the other cannot be brought into holes and cracks." Nothing could be clearer or more practical. Only a light that is small enough to fit into the most hidden recesses will be effective in illuminating where we are going, where we are searching, literally and figuratively.

Rabbi Zebid says: "The one [the candle/lamp, throws] its light forward, whereas the other [throws] its light behind." The sparks of divinity within us reach forward to reunite with the great light of the divine; the great light of the divine is always reaching backward to us. A torch, says Rabbi Zebid, throws the bulk of its light backward as it is lowered, whereas a candle's light is not powerful enough for that movement to affect its light.

Rabbi Papa adds: "Here [with a torch] one is afraid, whereas there [with a the lamp/candle] one is not afraid"—that is, with a torch we might hesitate to look closely for fear of setting the house on fire, but not so with a candle/lamp. Philosophically, the light of the divine is too terrifying, whereas the spark of the divine is sufficient to embolden us to begin to search our ways.

And Rabina concludes the discussion: "The light of the one [the candle/lamp] is steady, whereas that of the other is fitful"—that is, the larger torch shakes in our hand, and its larger flame throws an unsteady light. The spark of the divine within us, however, is manageable—but the flame of God Himself is beyond our ability to control.

And so, when we reach the end of the gemara's discussion, we find that the law of the mishnah—that a candle/lamp must be used to search for ḥametz—has been maintained. But along the way we have engaged in a far-reaching discussion of the theology of a symbolic search. We have learned that leaven is a symbol of the proclivity of humans to act against one another. It is a symbol for the evil that, the prophet Zephaniah cautions us, will lead to our destruction. And we have learned much about the nature of light: that the light within us is the source of our ability to act righteously and is but a spark of God, a much greater light, the source of all light. The light within us is not the fullness of God's light—that is beyond our ability to contain—but God's light awaits us in a redeemed world that some day will be ushered in by Pesaḥ—when we have searched for, found, and destroyed all of the ḥametz. Only then will we be guests at God's "sacrificial feast."

LIFE, DEATH AND DOING THE LAUNDRY

Mishnah Ta'anith 26b
Gemara Ta'anith 29b

TEXT

Mishnah

With the beginning of Av rejoicings are curtailed. During the week in which the Ninth of Av falls, it is forbidden to cut hair and to wash clothes, but on Thursday it is permissible in honor of the Sabbath. On the eve of the Ninth of Av one may not partake of a meal of two courses nor eat meat nor drink wine. Rabbi Simeon ben Gamaliel said: One should make a difference in his diet. Rabbi Judah makes it obligatory to turn the bed over; the sages, however did not agree with him in this.

Gemara

Rabbi Hamnuna raised an objection: "On Thursday it is permissible in honor of the Sabbath." What is permissible? Shall I say it is to wash clothes for immediate wear? Where does the honor of the

Sabbath enter into it? It must surely mean, washing clothes for storing [until the Sabbath], and this is permissible only on Thursday but not on other days of the week! In reality [the mishnah refers] to the washing of clothes for immediate wear, and it speaks of a case in which a man has only one shirt. For, Rabbi Assi said in the name of Rabbi Yoḥanan: When a man has only one shirt, he may wash it on the intermediate days of the festival. So, too, it has been stated: Rabbi Benjamin said in the name of Rabbi Eleazar: The restriction applies only to washing clothes for immediate wear but washing clothes for storing is permissible. An objection was raised against this: It is forbidden to wash clothes before the Ninth of Av even for storing them until after the Ninth of Av. And our [Babylonian] laundry work is like their [Palestinian] plain washing [in respect of this prohibition], but flaxen garments are not included in this prohibition against laundry work. This is indeed a refutation.

INTERPRETATION

The ninth day of the Hebrew month of Av has been observed with profound sadness by the Jewish people for nearly two millennia. Tradition recounts that on this date in 586 B.C.E. the Temple in Jerusalem was destroyed, and on this date in 70 C.E. the rebuilt Second Temple in Jerusalem was also destroyed. It is a day of national mourning, characterized by the same debilitating grief we experience when we lose a loved one.

The week leading up to the Ninth of Av is, by tradition, already laden with sadness, culminating on Tisha b'Av, the Ninth of Av, in a full fast day, during which one assumes all of the restrictions normally incumbent on a mourner. Tisha b'Av itself is like *shivah*, the seven days of personal mourning, rolled into one day. The week preceding Tisha b'Av is equivalent to the *sheloshim*, the thirty days of mourning following a funeral. The beginning of the month of Av itself has the equivalent weight of the twelve months of mourning that usually follow the death of a parent. Unlike personal mourning, during which our grief diminishes over time, the opposite is true of Tisha b'Av: our grief builds toward the fast day.

We are not surprised, then, that the mishnah teaches that, with the beginning of Av, rejoicing is curtailed. Nor are we surprised that cutting one's hair and washing one's clothes, activities associated with preparing for special joyous occasions and curtailed during mourning, are similarly curtailed in the week before the fast. Mourners should have no vain concerns about their appearances. Finally, we are not surprised that these restrictions are lifted on a Thursday in order to allow us to prepare for the Sabbath, for public mourning is suspended on the Sabbath. Unlike the other full fast day of the Jewish year, Yom Kippur, Tisha b'Av itself is not observed on the Sabbath; if the ninth day of Av falls on a Sabbath, the fast is observed on the following day.

In the gemara, however, the seemingly straightforward regulations promulgated by the mishnah become the catalyst for a much deeper discussion concerning the relationship between the darkest moment of life, death, and the brightest moment of life, the promise of life without death. The former is represented by Tisha b'Av; the latter, by the Sabbath; and the two are tied together somehow by the act of washing clothes.

Our passage in the gemara begins by raising an objection to the law as stated in the mishnah. Rabbi Hamnuna asks: What exactly is permitted, and why? If it is permissible to wash clothes for immediate wear on Thursday, then how can the text claim that the honor of the Sabbath is involved? On the other hand, if it is permissible to wash clothes only in order to store them until the Sabbath, then why not permit doing so on any day of the week? Why only on Thursday? The gemara answers this latter objection by explaining that the mishnah's proviso applies only in a case in which the person has but one shirt to wear!

Suddenly, the context of our discussion has shifted. No longer are we concerned with the honor of the Sabbath. Rather we are concerned with the honor of a human being. How does the text accomplish this shift in context? Rabbi Assi quotes a teaching in the name of Rabbi Yoḥanan: "When a man has only one shirt, he may wash it on the intermediate days of the festival." On those festival days on which washing clothes is usually prohibited because the drudgery involved detracts from the celebratory spirit, doing laundry is, nevertheless, permitted if one has only one shirt to wear—that is, the honor of a human being takes precedence over the honor of the festival. Similarly, the honor of a human being takes precedence over the honor of the Sabbath.

Let us reflect on where this brief passage of Talmud has already taken us. We began with the mishnah's working assumption that during the quasi-mourning period preceding Tisha b'Av, washing clothes is prohibited. National tragedy is thus analogized to personal grief. We are asked to respond to the destruction of the Temple as we would respond to the death of a parent, spouse, or child. Even though we are to equate national tragedy to personal tragedy, however, the mishnah reminds us that personal mourning must be interrupted for purposes of national/communal celebrating! Indeed, one of the most difficult, yet most therapeutic, rules of Jewish mourning is that it is suspended by the Sabbath and superseded by the festivals. Understanding this spiritual hierarchy within Jewish practice helps us understand the gemara's question, "Where does the honor of the Sabbath enter into it?" Although we are here ostensibly discussing the destruction of Jerusalem and the Holy Temple, we need to be reminded that in individual mourning, the community takes precedence over personal concerns. Perhaps the Sabbath's role as giving us a taste of the world to come—the world without death—serves to elevate us beyond personal grief. But the Temple was the very agency that ensured the observance of Sabbath and festivals! Without the Temple, how can one properly honor the Sabbath?

The gemara teaches us that it is precisely when structures of meaning have broken down, when the avenues of redemptive rituals seem unavailable, that we need to move beyond the honor of the Sabbath to concern ourselves with the honor of human beings, those left with only the shirt on their backs. We need to be reminded that, while we busy ourselves mourning for Jerusalem, others worry about doing their laundry so as not to walk the streets shirtless.

The gemara demands that we ask ourselves: Which is more important, honoring the Sabbath or concerning ourselves about the minimal comforts of our fellow human beings? In the wake of the destruction of Israel's ritual center, how do we begin the process of restoration and reconciliation?—with ritual or with good works? These questions once confronted the masters of the gemara, and they now confront us with equal urgency. We might conclude from this part of the discussion that the gemara opts for people over ritual, but that would be facile. Complex questions cannot be given simplistic answers. The gemara in general rejects such totalization, the either-or thinking implicit in Western philosophy. Typically, the gemara guides us through complexity by helping us to recognize that there is a tension between either-or propositions. Sometimes the answer is both.

Rabbi Benjamin, in the name of Rabbi Eleazar, returns us to our argument. He reasserts the proposition that during the week of Tisha b'Av one may not wash clothes on a Thursday just because one needs clean clothes that day, but only in order to have clean clothes to wear on the Sabbath, or even for after Tisha b'Av itself. Stubbornly, the gemara continues to hold that both the honor of the Sabbath and concern for the daily needs of the poor are appropriate responses to the destruction of the Temple. Yet, perhaps, one cannot have it both ways. Nevertheless, to have it only one way is simply unacceptable. And so, once more, the gemara objects.

We are now presented with a teaching that forbids washing clothes even in order to store them for the Sabbath. In raising this tradition, the gemara apparently experiments with the possibility of concluding that neither honoring the Sabbath—that is, ritual—nor honoring human beings will suffice to dispel our grief for the Temple's loss. However, the gemara refutes this notion by drawing a distinction between the laundry work done in Palestine and that done in Babylonia. In Palestine, we learn, "plain" washing of clothes is prohibited. This "plain" washing is equivalent to the finer type of laundry work done in Babylonia—the kind of laundry work reserved for the finer garments of the rich. But the flaxen garments worn by the poor are not to be included in this prohibition! Thus, the gemara itself refutes the notion that neither the Sabbath nor our acts of concern for the poor can stay our grief.

We are, therefore, left with a complex answer to a complex question. We cannot simply declare that no answer is possible, nor can we affirm that only one way—either ritual or ethics—will suffice to express our grief. We reject the notion that grieving is endless, but we recognize somewhat reluctantly that we owe our respite from grief primarily to our vantage point in exile, in Babylonia. In Israel it might be appropriate to grieve inconsolably. We learn that even in exile, washing clothes, a symbol of normal life and expectations, is prohibited before Tisha b'Av but that, for the immediate needs of the poor, it is permitted. For the honor of the Sabbath, even washing clothes and storing them is permitted. Both ethics and ritual have become the building blocks of our response to tragedy and exile. The Sabbath is the balm that eases the mourning and offers us the transcendence over death once offered by the Temple. But for the poor this palliative is insufficient. They are also allowed to wash their clothes and wear them, for, if the law cannot accommodate itself to their needs, then no salvation is possible. It was precisely this balance among the agency of ritual, restoration, and the reconciliation that derives from our commitment to others' needs that brought Israel beyond mourning to comfort two thousand years ago and today offers us a strong model for a generation faced with a similar predicament.

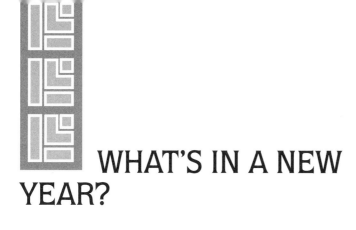

WHAT'S IN A NEW YEAR?

Rosh Hashanah 2a, 2b

TEXT

Mishnah

There are four new years. On the first of Nisan is the new year for kings and for festivals. On the first of Elul is the new year for the tithe of cattle. Rabbi Eleazar and Rabbi Simeon, however, place this on the first of Tishrei. On the first of Tishrei is the new year for years: for release and jubilee years, for planting and for [tithe of] vegetables. On the first of Shevat is the new year for trees, according to the ruling of Beit Shammai; Beit Hillel, however, places it on the fifteenth of that month.

Gemara

Rabbi Yoḥanan said: How do we know [from the Scriptures] that the years of kings' reigns are always reckoned as commencing from Nisan? Because it says, "In the four hundred and eightieth year after the Israelites left the land of Egypt, in the fourth year of Solomon's reign over Israel, in the month of Ziv—that is, the second month" (I Kings 6:1). Here Solomon's reign is put side by side with the Exodus from Egypt [to indicate that] just as [the years from] the Exodus from Egypt are reckoned from Nisan, so [the years of] Solomon's reign commenced with Nisan.

But how do we know that the years from the Exodus from Egypt itself are reckoned as commencing with Nisan? Perhaps we reckon them from Tishrei? Do not imagine such a thing. For it is written, "Aaron the priest ascended Mount Hor at the command of the LORD and died there, in the fortieth year after the Israelites had left the land of Egypt, on the first day of the fifth month" (Num. 33:38), and it is further written, "It was in the fortieth year, on the first day of the eleventh month, that Moses addressed . . . " (Deut. 11:3), and so on. Now, since the text, when referring to Av, places it in the fortieth year, and again when referring to [the following] Shevat, places it also in the fortieth year, we may conclude that Tishrei is not the beginning of the year. [This, however] is not conclusive. I grant you that the former text states explicitly that [the year spoken of was] "after the Israelites had left the land of Egypt"; but how do we know that [the year mentioned in] the latter text is reckoned from the Exodus? Perhaps it is from the setting up of the Tabernacle. [We may reply to this] on the model of Rabbi Papa, who said [in another connection] that the occurrence of the expression "twentieth year" in two contexts provides us with a *gezerah shavah*: so here, [I may say that the occurrence of] the expression "fortieth year" in the two contexts provides us with a *gezerah shavah*, [showing that] just as in the one case [the date is reckoned] from the Exodus, so in the other case also.

INTERPRETATION

Among the primary functions of religious life is to give meaning to time. From the perspective of infinity it is not important whether today is Monday or Wednesday, whether this is the first month or the seventh, but from the perspective of Shabbat, it matters a great deal whether there are five days of preparation left or three; and from the perspective of dating a check, getting married, remembering a birthday or the anniversary of a death, it matters greatly what the month is. In other words, everything that is important to us occurs in time; marking that time appropriately is part of affirming what is important to us and preserving it in memory.

Although the year is not our smallest unit of time, it can be considered the building block of time because it contains one full cycle of those events that move us further from our beginning, closer to our end. It contains the four seasons, as well as the shortest and longest periods of daylight and darkness. In every culture, among every people, the natural rhythm of the year is accepted as a given point of reference. The year's beginning, the New Year, is not only an important occasion in itself; each culture's choice of when to begin the year can also tell us something about the values of those doing the choosing.

The mishnah before you describes four Jewish new years. Having several new years is not unusual; most cultures have overlapping calendars. In the United States, for instance, we have a fiscal year, a school year, a tax year, and the so-called calendar year. But it is not the details elaborated in the mishnah on this subject that concern us here. Rather, we are going to look at the talmudic passage attached to this mishnah, whose topic grows out of the mishnah but moves beyond an investigation into its details. This passage explores the meaning of a New Year.

The mishnah established that the first of Nisan is the New Year of Kings—that is, the date from which the years of a king's reign are reckoned, what we might call the political year. Rabbi Yoḥanan asks for the biblical justification for such an assertion. He answers with a verse from the First Book of Kings (6:1). Since the event in question in the chapter is dated both by the years of the king's reign and the Exodus from Egypt, we are to conclude that the month of the Exodus from Egypt, Nisan, is ostensibly the month from which the years of the king's reign should be dated. But talmudic study requires that we investigate the full context of biblical verses quoted before we jump to conclusions. Often what is not part of the quotation is as important as what is. And we also must investigate the background of the rabbi doing the quoting. Often his particular orientation to larger issues plays a role in a particular discussion.

Chapter 6 of I Kings describes the construction of Solomon's Temple. The chapter begins with the date that we have quoted and ends with a dating that mentions the king's reign but not the Exodus. No other dates occur in the description of Solomon's reign. Although the spans of various royal reigns are mentioned throughout the Book of Kings, no other date but this one is juxtaposed to the years since the Exodus from Egypt. All of them, like the concluding date in chapter 6, mention only the number of years of the king's reign. Rabbi Yoḥanan would have assumed our familiarity with the context of this passage. A second generation Palestinian *Amora* (teacher) of the highest stature, he was renowned as a halakhist (legalist) and as a teacher of aggadah (nonlegal material). Among his specialties in aggadah (lore) were stories dealing with quasi-historical recountings of the period of the destruction of the Second Temple in Jerusalem. Many of his *aggadot* memorialize the heroes of that period and explain the causes of the destruction as well. In that light, then, we should not be surprised that he identifies the counting of political years both with the initial act of historical redemption, the Exodus from Egypt, and with the construction of the Temple in Jerusalem. We might say, even at this early juncture in our exposition of the text, that to the Talmud, political time, the time we are most familiar with in our everyday lives and to which we feel most beholden, is itself afforded meaning only in terms of redemption and through the concrete expression of redemption in the unredeemed world, the Temple.

The difference between redemption and time is the difference between life and death. To be more specific, time in our world measures life in its march toward death; redemption points toward a world in which death has been overcome. The meaning of time, therefore, ordinary political time, is found in the relationship between these two dimensions. Time in this world is the measurement of a journey toward death; redemptive time is the anticipated *experience* of a world where death is conquered. Without this anticipated conquest of death, time in this world loses its meaning because death unconquered destroys all meaning. But redemption, we learn by implication, has two forms: an ideal form, represented by the Exodus from Egypt, and a concrete form, represented by the Temple in Jerusalem (and by analogy, the Tabernacle that was constructed in the wilderness).

The next part of our talmudic passage explores the differences between dating events from the ideal redemption of the Exodus and dating them from the concrete realization of redemption, the Temple. These differences are framed in the guise of an argument between those who support the logic of counting the years since the Exodus from the New Year of Nisan and those who would count the years since the Exodus from the New Year of Tishrei.

TEXT

But how do we know that the years from the Exodus from Egypt itself are reckoned as commencing with Nisan? Perhaps we reckon them from Tishrei? Do not imagine such a thing. For it is written, "Aaron the priest ascended Mount Hor at the command of the

LORD and died there, in the fortieth year after the Israelites had left the land of Egypt, on the first day of the fifth month" (Num. 33:38), and it is further written, "It was in the fortieth year, on the first day of the eleventh month, that Moses addressed . . . " (Deut. 11:3), and so on. Now, since the text, when referring to Av, places it in the fortieth year, and again when referring to [the following] Shevat, places it also in the fortieth year, we may conclude that Tishrei is not the beginning of the year.

INTERPRETATION

The question with which the Talmud begins this part of the discussion concerns the counting of the years from the Exodus itself. Should they be reckoned from the month of Nisan or from the month of Tishrei? The answer—from Nisan—is construed to be obvious: "Do not imagine such a thing"; it is based on two more biblical verses, which we must again look at closely.

On the surface, the question is answered based on simple logic. Since both verses, one from Numbers and one from Deuteronomy, date events as being forty years from the Exodus and since the months of Av and Shevat are calculated to be in the same year, Tishrei, which comes between them, could not begin a new year. Hence, Nisan must be the New Year. Once again, the context of the verses quoted is informative. The verse in Numbers describes the death of Aaron in the course of a recapitulation of the travels of the people of Israel since the Exodus. The verse in Deuteronomy introduces the recapitulation of history and law preliminary to the death of Moses.

First, we must ask ourselves whether a difference between the Nisan date and the Tishrei date has emerged and what that difference is. If, as is quite clear, Nisan begins the new year on the basis of its association with redemption, on what basis do we even suggest that Tishrei is a New Year? First of all, we must now return to the mishnah. If both the political year and the cycle of festivals begin in Nisan because of its association with redemption, then Tishrei must be the New Year for the counting of the sabbatical years and the jubilee years; for determining the ritual permissibility of planted fruit; and for the tithes of vegetables and, at least according to rabbis Eleazar and Simeon, the tithe of cattle too. All of these functions are tied to the rituals associated with the Temple. Thus, the distinction we have previously made between redemption and the agency of redemption in an unredeemed world, between the Exodus and the Temple, is, in fact, the difference between new years. Nisan is the ideal New Year; Tishrei, the real New Year.

Returning to the text of our passage in the Talmud, we have two questions yet to explore. First, regarding Nisan, if it is the ideal New Year, why do we not celebrate it as such, transferring all the solemnity of Rosh Hashanah to the first of Nisan? Second, what is the relationship between the New Year of Nisan and the New Year of Tishrei? When we have answered these questions, we can ask our final question: What framework of meaning do we as contemporary Jews take from this discussion?

Why does the Talmud introduce the biblical selections from Numbers and Deuteronomy? Ostensibly to prove that we reckon the years since the Exodus from Nisan. But is such a proof necessary? Since the Exodus is construed to be an actual event, an event in time, under what circumstances could we imagine not dating an event from when it occurred? None. The particular biblical verses must have another purpose, a purpose connected both to the death of Aaron and the conclusion of Moses' mission. I suggest that that purpose is to alert us to the fact that the redemption promised by the Exodus from Egypt, the redemption delayed by the wandering in the wilderness, the redemption characterized as the habitation of the land of Israel, political redemption, freedom from slavery, is not the final redemption but a conditional, mortal, transitory redemption. Aaron's death symbolizes the suspension of the miraculous divine protection of Israel that began at the Red Sea. Moses' iteration of the law by way of farewell was a transfer of hope from the Nisan of forty years before to a future to be characterized by law and ritual. Nisan would have been our New Year had Aaron and Moses not been destined to die. Tishrei is our New Year in the world that follows their death, a world in which redemption is a desire and law and ritual the path to attaining our desire.

However, the Temple has been destroyed. This seemingly obvious statement must here be emphasized. If the interpretation of the mishnah offered by the gemara is, as I believe, a philosophic exploration of the difference between the ideal world and the real world as expressed in time, then it must be kept in mind that the crisis confronted by both the mishnah and the talmudic commentary is not merely the theoretic distinction between an ideal world and a real world, but the far more poignant distinction between a real world and a real world destroyed. If the world is already a faint image of a long lost ideal, how do we live when that image itself is broken? We no longer long for redemption; that is too far away. We long for a world in which we could dare to hope for redemption. This was the world of the Talmud. This is the world of today.

TEXT

[This, however] is not conclusive. I grant you that the former text states explicitly that [the year spoken of was] "after the Israelites had left the land of Egypt"; but how do we know that [the year mentioned in] the latter text is reckoned from the Exodus? Perhaps it is from the setting up of the Tabernacle. [We may reply to this] on the model of Rabbi Papa, who said [in another connection] that the occurrence of the expression "twentieth year" in two contexts provides us with a *gezerah shavah:* so here, [I may say that the occurrence of] the expression "fortieth year" in the two contexts provides us with a *gezerah shavah,* [showing that] just as in the one case [the date is reckoned] from the Exodus, so in the other case also.

INTERPRETATION

We return one last time to our text, sensitive to the context we have established above—that is, this *sugya* continues to unfold against a backdrop of a world, and its symbols of redemption, destroyed. We rejoin the text with the words: "[This, however] is not conclusive"—that is, the passages from Numbers and Deuteronomy are not absolutely analogous. In one, the description of the death of Aaron, the Exodus is mentioned explicitly, but in the verse from Deuteronomy it is not. Perhaps in the latter case the beginning of the year should be considered Tishrei after all? "Perhaps it is from the setting up of the Tabernacle?"

With this question the gemara establishes explicitly the contrast between the New Year based on the redemption from Egypt and the New Year based on the raising of the Tabernacle or Temple. In the superficial terms of the argument, this reference to the Tabernacle is not intended to stand for Tishrei. On the contrary, the Tabernacle, too, was erected in Nisan; but if the Nisan intended by this verse is the Nisan of the setting up of the Tabernacle, that occurred in the second year of the Exodus. The two verses, then, would not be analogous; one would date Aaron's death counting from the time of the Exodus, whereas the other would date the beginning of Moses' farewell counting from the year after the Exodus, from the establishment of the Tabernacle. If this were the case then the new years of Nisan and Tishrei would not be related at all. Redemption and sacrifice would be of no relation to one another. The ideal New Year would be incommensurate with the real New Year. If this were so when the Temple stood, how much more so when the Temple was destroyed. If redemption and worship have no relationship to each other, then our Rosh Hashanah worship could offer us no hope of effecting any change in the status quo. It would be an empty service. This is the true subject of the Talmud's discussion here. After the Exodus failed to provide ultimate redemption, did the Temple in Jerusalem provide at least a hope for redemption? If it did not, no further questions need be asked. If it did, then the destruction of the Temple poses a problem: how to provide a hope for redemption in its absence; but it is not necessarily an insoluble problem.

The gemara provides an answer in the form of a paradigm for studying Torah, the *gezerah shavah,* a rhetorical device positing that when two verses contain the same phrase, the meaning of the first phrase in its entirety can be ascribed to the second occurrence of that phrase by a "verbal analogy." This technical solution resolves all of our philosophic and theological questions along with the "superficial" halakhic question: Which New Year is when?

Here is the beauty of Talmud study—and its profound difficulty. While the Talmud often provides simple answers to questions no one is really interested in, it usually provides only approaches to answering questions people really are interested in. Yet, though this method can be frustrating, it is brutally honest. For, the difficult questions in philosophy and in life rarely have simple, direct answers.

Rabbi Papa "proves" that both verses quoted by the Talmud, the one from Numbers and the one from Deuteronomy, refer to the same Nisan, the same year, the same Exodus, the same redemption. He does so by claiming that rabbinic rules of Torah interpretation tell us what scripture *means* regardless of what it *says.* He demonstrates the power of *talmud Torah,* Torah study, to continue the process of hearing God's voice in the world. He enwraps the Exodus and the Temple together in rabbinic hermeneutics, thereby redefining both redemption and worship as study. In so doing he answers Rabbi Yoḥanan's true question: Without a Temple in which to worship, how can we pray for a potential redemption at the New Year of Tishrei that might someday renew the ideal redemption at the New Year of Nisan? The answer implied by our gemara is: Study is the vehicle for continuing to seek redemption in a still unredeemed world bereft of the Temple. Such is the meaning of Rosh Hashanah—our Rosh Hashanah of Tishrei: It is the New Year of study, through which we strive to hasten redemption.

PROPHECY, SACRIFICE, AND SUFFERING

Sanhedrin 89a and 89b

TEXT

Mishnah

"A false prophet": One who prophesies what he has not heard, or what was not told to him, is executed by man; but one who suppresses his prophecy, or disregards the words of a prophet, or a prophet who transgresses his own words—his death is at the hands of heaven, for it is written, "[And one who fails to heed the words which he speaks in My name,] I myself will call him to account" (Deut. 18:19).

Gemara

"One who disregards the words of a prophet." But how does he know that he should be punished? If he gives him a sign. But Micah did not give a sign, yet he was punished! (I Kings 20:35) If he was well established [as a prophet], it is different. For, should you not admit this, how could Isaac listen to Abraham at Mount Moriah, or the people listen to Elijah at Mount Carmel and sacrifice without [the Temple]? Hence the case in which the prophet is well established is different.

"Some time afterward God put Abraham to the test" (Gen. 22:1). What is meant by "after"? Rabbi Yoḥanan said on the authority of Rabbi Yose ben Zimra: "After" the words of Satan, as it is written, "The child grew up and was weaned, [and Abraham held a great feast on the day that Isaac was weaned"] (Gen. 21:8). Thereupon, Satan said to the Almighty: "Sovereign of the Universe! To this old man You graciously gave the fruit of the womb at the age of a hundred, yet of all that banquet which he prepared, he did not have one turtledove or pigeon to sacrifice before you! Has he done anything but in honor of his son!" Replied He, "Yet were I to say to him, 'Sacrifice your son before Me,' he would do so without hesitation." Straightway, "God put Abraham to the test. . . . And He said 'Take, I pray you [na] your son.'" Rabbi Simeon ben Abba said: na can only denote entreaty. This may be compared to a king of flesh and blood who was confronted by many wars, which he won by the aid of a great warrior. Subsequently, he was faced with a severe battle. Thereupon, he said to him, "I pray you, assist me in battle, that people may not say, there was no reality in the earlier ones." So also did the Holy One, blessed be He, say unto Abraham, "I have tested you with many trials and you withstood them all. Now, be firm for My sake in this trial, that men may not say, there was no reality in the earlier ones."

"Your son."

[But] I have two sons!

"Your only one."

Each is the only one of his mother!

"Whom you love."

I love them both!

"Isaac!"

And why all this [circumlocution]? So that his mind should not reel [under the sudden shock].

On the way Satan came toward him and said to him, "If we try to commune with you, will you be grieved? . . . Behold, you have instructed many, and you have strengthened the weak hands. Your words have upheld him that was falling, and you have strengthened the feeble knees. But now it is come upon you, and you failed the test." He replied, "I will walk in my integrity." "But," said [Satan] to him, "should not your fear be your confidence?" "Remember," he retorted, "I pray you, whoever perished being innocent?" Seeing that he would not listen to him, he said to him, "Now a thing was secretly brought to me: thus have I heard from behind the Curtain, 'The lamb, for a burnt offering but not Isaac for a burnt offering.'" He replied, "It is the penalty of a liar, that should he even tell the truth, he is not listened to."

INTERPRETATION

People say all the time: What if Moses came down today and said, "Do this or that"? No one would listen; such a prophet would be "put away." Substitute for Moses Jesus, Buddha, or Mohammed, and we reach the same conclusion: nowadays prophecy is only something we read about in books. Anyone claiming prophetic power today would— and we would probably agree, *should*— be scorned.

The mishnah and gemara you have before you deal with this crucial issue, both as it plays out in the prophetic past and as it might unfold in the potential prophetic future. These texts, in fact, consider the most frightening prophetic vision possible, a murder whose provenience is ascribed to God's will. In taking up this issue, the Talmud is faced with a difficult conundrum: on the one hand, religion depends upon the possibility of prophecy; on the other hand, the society in which religion is expected to function is fundamentally threatened by the destabilizing activities of prophets and prophecy.

It is in this context that we as a community encounter *akedat Yitzḥak*— the Binding of Isaac—at the New Year. We, too, understand, especially at this time of year, the need for us and our religion to be "shaken up," to be stirred from our complacency by a renewed prophetic call, summoning us to justice and compassion. At the same time, we are aware that tomorrow is another day. We resist having the very foundations of our daily lives exposed to the prophet's sharp critique. We require routine, even some protective callousness. For us, as for the Rabbis, *akedat Yitzḥak* is a paradox. Its pure prophetic faith simultaneously inspires and frightens us.

What can we do? The mishnah suggests that both the prophets and their audience are governed by law—that is, the primary vehicle of revelation, according to the Rabbis, is not the inspired voice of the prophet, but the continuing interpretation of God's voice, publicly revealed at Sinai. The prophetic voice is a legitimate *other* mode of revelation, a subservient mode.

The mishnah then details the punishment meted out against someone who disregards the words of a prophet. The gemara immediately
raises the obvious problem inherent in this mishnah: "How does he
know that he is a true prophet so that disregarding him would mean liability to punishment?" The gemara answers its own question: a true
prophet gives a sign. The gemara then raises an apparent exception to
its own rule by citing an incident in I Kings 20:35 in which a prophet
(unnamed in the Bible but identified by the Rabbis as Micah or Micaiah
ben Imlah) orders one of his companions to assault him with a sword,
claiming such an act has been ordained "at the word of the Lord."
When the companion refuses, presumably unsure that such an act, obviously forbidden by law, is sanctioned by God through prophecy, the
prophet curses his companion, prophesying that since he disregarded
the word of a prophet he will be slain by a lion. Because this punishment comes to pass and despite the fact that the prophet had given no
sign, the gemara's objection is thereby refuted.

The gemara's choice of this particular incident for its argument sets
the context for the discussion of *akedat Yitzhak* that follows. We have encountered here the dark underside of prophecy. The reason this prophet
wants to be wounded is to teach King Ahab a lesson about divine justice. Although Ahab had been himself commanded by God to kill Ben-
hadad after their battle, he had failed to do so and, therefore, himself
merited death. Even though divinely ordained murder is the most
destabilizing and difficult prophecy any human being can follow, it is
precisely Ahab's avoidance of such murder or similar violence that
makes him liable for death—a fate shared by the prophet's companion,
who refuses a similar charge. These passages must surely trouble us
and in fact place the whole institution of prophecy in doubt, but it is
just such doubt that the Talmud wants to explore: Is all prophecy an ex-
cuse for murder? We will later return to this question.

The gemara now comes back to its original question: How do we
know a real prophet so that we can be sure not to disregard his words? If
he need not give us a sign, then how will we know? The gemara answers:
"If he was well established as a prophet it is different." As undisputed
proof, we are presented with the cases of Isaac and Elijah. Isaac allows
his father to bind him as a sacrifice, and the people allow Elijah to perform sacrifices outside the Temple, only because these two men are recognized by people as well-established prophets. The gemara appears to
accept this criterion as legitimate for judging the authenticity of a prophet;
disregarding such a prophet would make one liable to punishment.

Yet this is not an adequate answer. For, what if the prophet is just starting out in his mission? Is it then permitted to disregard him? What constitutes being "well established"? How many years? How successful must he be? Here the gemara is uncharacteristically silent. The focus now changes to Abraham and his binding of Isaac on the altar. I suggest that this change of focus is not coincidental and that it represents more than merely a link in the chain of random associations. Rather the exegetical re-creation of the *akedat Yitzḥak* is intended to "answer" the gemara's earlier question: How do we recognize a true prophet?

In the Torah, the narrative of *akedat Yitzḥak* begins with the assertion that all that follows is a test. We, the readers, are aware that God is testing Abraham. What is not immediately known, however, is what is being tested. Faith? Courage? Obedience? All are possibilities; all have been invoked by way of explanation throughout the centuries. I would like to suggest that, in the context of our gemara, this event is also a test of Abraham's claim to be a true prophet.

The gemara begins by asking about the word "after" in the verse: "Some time afterward [literally, "After these words/things"] God put Abraham to the test" (Gen. 22:1). What is being referred to by the words "after these words"? Rabbi Yoḥanan answers on the authority of Rabbi Yose ben Zimra that the text is referring to a conversation between God and Satan, *after* which Abraham is tested. Before we look at this conversation, we must explore the context of the biblical verses forming the skeleton of the exegesis. Our passage is constructed around nine verses from the Tanakh—four from Genesis, four from Job, and one from the Psalms. Before looking at the verses in detail, however, some general remarks are in order about the gemara's juxtaposition of Job and the *akedah*.

The fourth chapter of Job follows immediately after Job stoically withstands all the calamities God heaps upon him at Satan's urging. He has repeatedly refused to speak out against God; he has sat on the ground for seven days and seven nights in the company of his three friends; and he has finally cursed the day of his birth. He also has questioned God's reasons: "Why does He give light to the sufferer and life to the bitter in spirit?" In response to Job's complaint, Eliphaz the Temanite reminds Job that when others have been in trouble, Job has instructed and strengthened them, but now that trouble has come upon him, he is unable to withstand it. In the gemara, Satan quotes Eliphaz's words to Abraham.

Why would the gemara introduce Job's anguish into the story of Abraham? That Satan should quote Eliphaz is, perhaps, not surprising.

After all, Eliphaz represents the sort of conventional figure of consolation that the Book of Job itself rejects as illegitimate in the face of inexplicable evil afflicting good people. But why intertwine the two stories at all? The gemara is here beginning to construct the image of what I will call the wounded prophet—that is, in answer to our question: "How does one know an established prophet?" the gemara will explore the tension between prophecy and suffering. With this in mind, we turn to the text.

"Some time afterward God put Abraham to the test." We should not underestimate the centrality of this verse to the ensuing discussion in the gemara. We must also acknowledge the context of suffering to which we have just alluded. Indeed, the very purpose of this story is to cause Abraham to suffer! For, his prophetic standing cannot be affirmed until he has withstood this suffering.

Is there a justification for this test? According to Satan there is. Quoting from Genesis 21:8, Satan points out that when Isaac was weaned, Abraham made a great feast to celebrate, but did not offer any sacrifice of thanksgiving to God. According to Satan, Abraham's selfish happiness caused him to ignore God at an important moment. He is, therefore, not worthy of being God's messenger. It is in response to Abraham's selfish oversight that God orders the test: "And He said, 'Take [pray thee (*na*)] your son.'"

Here we have a slight digression and a parable. But digressions and parables are never slight in talmudic discourse. In fact, they are often the very heart of the matter. This parable is no exception. It is offered in the name of Rabbi Simeon ben Abba, who was of the family of the famous teacher, Samuel. Simeon was born in Babylonia, studied in Israel, and was impoverished all his life. Nothing he did to make a living succeeded. Rabbi Yoḥanan used to apply to him the verse, "Nor is bread won by the wise [scholars]" (Eccl. 9:11). He also said of him, "Anyone who knows the deeds of Abraham knows the deeds of this one's [Rabbi Simeon's] ancestors, yet the merit of his ancestors is no help to him" (J. Bikkurim, chap. 3, halakhah 3). Simeon was also very unfortunate in his personal affairs. He married twice, but both wives died soon after their marriages. Simeon was a respected scholar—a recognized authority, especially, on the limits placed on learning secular (or Greek) thought! He was, above all, a keeper of the faith.

Knowing all this, we find the following parable all the more poignant. Rabbi Simeon informs us that the word *na* can only mean "entreaty"—that is, God's test of Abraham is not the cruel demand of a megalomaniac God but the poignant request of a God in need. In need of what? Our parable tells of a great warrior king faced with a difficult battle that he is afraid of losing. Losing this great battle would undermine his reputation despite his former victories; people might say they weren't real victories. Thus, God says to Abraham, "Though you have withstood many trials, people may doubt that they were real trials and, therefore, doubt that God is real, unless you withstand, for God, one last great test, a trial that could be attributed only to a great prophet of a great God."

Then who is being tested? According to Rabbi Simeon it is the very reputation of God, the warrior king of the parable, that is at stake in the prophet's suffering. When Abraham binds Isaac to the altar, the one being questioned is not Abraham or Isaac, but God. What will God do? Human beings must constantly ask this question in order for God to act in the world. When prophets suffer, afflict themselves like Micah, are afflicted like Job, confront the horror of murder like Abraham, the extremity of their situation forces them to abandon the comfortable conventions of thought and ask questions about God. Human suffering, prophetic suffering at least, forces God to prove himself. Through our pain, God is tested. It is easy to imagine the urgency of this viewpoint for Rabbi Simeon. It is an even more compelling viewpoint for the Rabbis of the gemara as they survey the history of Israel in exile.

Thus, we have advanced our understanding of how to characterize a true prophet: Such a person suffers so that others may ask, "Where is God?" This is no easy task for a prophet to take on. Indeed, it is a shocking vocation; it can even be shattering. The gemara records a brief conversation between God and Abraham during which God gently breaks the news to Abraham about his test of faith. Abraham fights the dawning truth about what he is being asked to do. Like all prophets, he does not want the job. His hesitation provides Satan with just the opening Satan needs.

Satan's challenge begins by acknowledging the prophet's agony. The prophet is most vulnerable in the context of his pain. Abraham has before him the classical prophetic dilemma: to give precedence to his own pain, or to respond to the need and pain of God. Abraham responds to the Adversary's challenge with a phrase from Psalm 26: "I will walk in my integrity." This short psalm and its use to interpret a sequence of verses from Job fully captures the themes of our passage:

> Vindicate me, O LORD,
>> for I have walked without blame;

I have trusted in the LORD;
I have not faltered.
Probe me, O LORD, *and try me,*
test my heart and mind,
for my eyes are on Your steadfast love;
I have set my course by it.
I do not consort with scoundrels,
or mix with hypocrites;
I detest the company of evil men,
and do not consort with the wicked;
I wash my hands in innocence,
and walk around Your altar,
raising my voice in thanksgiving,
and telling all Your wonders.
O LORD, I love Your temple abode,
the dwelling place of Your glory.
Do not sweep me away with sinners,
or [snuff out] my life with murderers,
Who have schemes at their fingertips,
and hands full of bribes.
But I walk without blame;
redeem me, have mercy on me!
My feet are on level ground,
In assemblies I will bless the LORD.

Even a casual reading of this psalm reveals its contextual connection with our passage. I have italicized those lines that are particularly striking. We might even construe this psalm as a transcript of Abraham's address to God before, during, and after the *akedah*. He asks to be tested! He volunteers to stand for God in the world. He describes the characteristics of a person poised to receive the gift of prophecy. He walks around the altar on which his son is bound, singing praise and thanks to God. He prays that his action be construed not as murder but as sacrifice. His moral stance creates a Temple capable of transforming death into life. (That this psalm directly precedes the psalm that is recited liturgically twice a day in the penitential month preceding Yom Kippur would certainly have been known to the writers of the gemara. The Rabbis would have appreciated that Psalm 26 precedes Psalm 27, just as the reading of *akedat Yitzhak* on Rosh Hashanah precedes Yom Kippur.)

Returning to our text, we find Abraham accosted once more by Satan, who taunts him: "Should not your fear be your confidence?"—that is, should not Abraham's wholehearted devotion to God *exempt* him of having to undergo such trials and suffering? Abraham answers, this time quoting from the Book of Job, "Think now, what innocent man ever perished?" (Job 4:7). The verse Eliphaz uses to placate Job becomes an eloquent statement of Abraham's willingness to accept his wrenching task. And now Satan at last gives up trying to persuade Abraham to abandon his faith. Instead, he reveals God's secret: that the *akedah* is only a test; he assures Abraham that a lamb will be sacrificed instead. As a last resort, Satan tries to make Abraham despair of his whole mission by telling him the truth: this test of faith is a sham. Abraham counters not with a biblical verse, but with a line of folk wisdom: "It is the penalty of a liar, that even should he tell the truth, he is not listened to."

We began with the question: How do we determine who is a prophet? Our passage ends by informing us that it is not enough for a would-be prophet to tell the truth *at this moment,* for it is sometimes the case that the truth can be enlisted in the service of a lie. Someone who tells the truth by telling people what they want to hear is not a prophet. He is a Satan, an adversary of truth. Rather, the prophet is one like Abraham, who willingly undertakes to answer God's plea, to fulfill God's need that one person suffer undeservedly so that others may confront the question of God's providence in their lives. Through the prophet's example, they would understand that service to God is not necessarily related to receiving a reward. Thus, the *akedah* is transformed from a simple test of Abraham's faith into a test of his ability to assume God's need. This is our interpretation of the gemara's reading of the original biblical passages juxtaposed one to another.

The prophet, by definition, is one who *is* disregarded; this disregard is the root of his suffering. But why, then, should punishment befall one who disregards a prophet? Obviously, to return to our mishnah, punishment comes, not from people and human justice, but only from God. Therefore, when we encounter a prophet, we face a risk. The prophet's success depends, in part, on our disregarding him or her, and yet, in doing so, we put our life on the line. Thus, religious life is no light matter. We are confronted by decisions that threaten our equilibrium however we decide. The knife of Abraham hangs over each of us; the prophet invites it. The rest of us either embrace him for his inviting it or reject him. Either course places us on the altar beside Isaac.

And thus we return to the question of murder. In a certain way, the gemara suggests, all prophets traffic in murder. The possibility of murder in the service of God, the risk of murder as the prophet's mission, shocks us out of our complacency. Prophets possess the passion to do God's will, even to murder, as described in Psalm 26. For this reason they must be controlled by law. As we prepare ourselves on Rosh Hashanah to repent and turn our lives around, we discover that pondering this subject—the troubling phenomenon of prophecy—braces us for the task.

THE PROBLEM OF THE ABSENT GOD

Yoma 53b–54a

TEXT

Mishnah

After the Ark had been taken away, there was a stone from the days of the earlier prophets, called the *shetiyah*, three fingers above the ground, on which he would place [the pan of burning coals].

INTERPRETATION

From its beginning until we join it here in the fifth chapter, and beyond, mishnah *Yoma* focuses on the dramatic and crucial preparations undergone by the High Priest so that he might correctly carry out his all-important mission as the representative of the House of Israel seeking atonement. It also describes in great detail the sequence of the atonement ritual. But why does the mishnah provide such a detailed description of a ritual that no longer could be performed by the time of the mishnah? Why doesn't it construct a substitute ritual for effecting

103

atonement? Shouldn't the mishnah be asking how to seek atonement without a Temple? Without a Holy City? Even in exile?

A more important question is: What does atonement mean to us in our world in which God appears to be absent?

The mishnah we are studying here interrupts an ongoing description of the Temple ritual. The previous mishnah describes that part of the ritual during which the High Priest stands before the Ark of the Covenant, between the curtain of the Ark and the curtain behind which is the Holy of Holies. In this space, with a fire pan in one hand and a ladle of incense in the other, he heaps the incense onto the fire pan resting on the bars of the staves upon which the Ark rests, thereby creating a great deal of smoke from which he then emerges and offers a short prayer. However, before moving on to the next step, our mishnah digresses, informing us that this procedure has changed from the days of the First Temple to the days of the Second Temple. For though the atonement ceremony proceeded in the Second Temple in the same way it had in the first, no Ark was present in the Second Temple! The Ark had not returned from exile. We will return later to this question of the Ark's fate. For now, it is sufficient to point out that the Ark was missing, that its absence constituted a weighty symbolic loss—for there God's presence was said to dwell—and that nonetheless the Ark continued unequivocally to play a role in the now flawed but rebuilt Temple.

The mishnah continues by explaining that beneath the Ark, in its place, there remained a stone from the time of David and Solomon, from the period of the First Temple. This stone, called the *shetiyah* ("foundation"), became the place upon which the High Priest rested his fire pan, instead of on the bars of the Ark. Though it was a small stone, only three fingerbreadths above the level ground, it had to suffice for the enactment of the Yom Kippur ritual.

Both this practice of using a foundation stone in place of the missing Ark and the mishnah's recording of this fact after having described the Yom Kippur ceremony in its ideal pre-exile state are direct responses to the larger question I have raised regarding the possibility for atonement without a Temple.

Since the mythic function of the Temple is its being the locus of God in the world, a Temple from which God is absent is, in a sense, a contradiction. Worshiping in such a Temple is theologically untenable. And what about worshiping when that Temple itself is destroyed, when God is either exiled or hidden? The gemara now considers the different consequences for us of having an exiled God versus a hidden God.

TEXT

Gemara

[The mishnah] does not teach, "After the Ark has been hidden away"; this is in accord with him who holds that the Ark went into exile to Babylonia, for it was taught: Rabbi Eliezer said: The Ark went into exile to Babylonia, as it was said: "At the turn of the year King Nebuchadnezzar sent and had him brought to Babylon together with the precious vessels of the house of the LORD" (II Chron. 36:10). Rabbi Simeon bar Yoḥai said: The Ark went into exile to Babylonia, as it was said: "Nothing will be left behind, said the LORD" (Isa. 39:6)—that is, the Ten Commandments contained therein. Rabbi Judah bar Ilai said: The Ark was hidden [buried] in its own place, as it was said: "The poles projected so that the ends of the poles were visible in the Sanctuary in front of the Shrine; but they could not be seen outside; and there they remain to this day" (I Kings 8:8). Now he disputes Ulla, for Ulla said: Rabbi Mattyah ben Ḥeresh asked Rabbi Simeon bar Yoḥai in Rome: "Now, Rabbi Eliezer taught us that on the first and second occasion the Ark went into exile to Babylonia. (The first was the one which we stated just now: And he 'had him brought to Babylon together with the precious vessels of the house of the LORD,' but what is the second one?)" It is written, "Gone from fair Zion [54a] are all that were her glory" (Lam. 1:6). What does "all her glory" mean? All that is enclosed within her.

INTERPRETATION

The gemara begins by noting what the mishnah does *not* teach: that God is in hiding. If, as it would seem, the fact of God's absence is taken for granted by the rabbinic authors, absence both from the Second Temple itself and, what is more important, from the post-Temple community, we can only conclude that they attribute this absence to the fact that Jerusalem lies in ruins (or that the Temple is not fully restored to its pre-exile state). God is absent not because God has gone into hiding. Why is this important? We must picture a community of Jews who feel, in no uncertain terms, abandoned by God. The leadership of such a community felt called upon to restore a sense of God's presence and concern for this community. But what could such a leadership offer by way of explanation?

For this devastated community and its leadership, the difference between a God in hiding and a God in exile is enormous. For an exiled God, one can only wait passively, and such a God's return depends upon the restoration of a place, a city, a temple. But a different kind of response is demanded when God has gone into hiding. A hidden God must be searched for. And we must entertain the possibility that we will never have more than scant evidence of this God's existence. It is a tall order to maintain faith in a God we cannot and may never be able to find. A God in exile is still with God's people; a God in hiding is absent. Yet, these were the only choices before both the mishnaic and talmudic sages. I suggest that they are also our choices: we can either wait for the old God to return or search for a God whom we may never find.

The mishnah and the gemara agree that God is in exile. The gemara specifically insists that the mishnah *does not* teach that God is hidden, but specifically that God is in exile. For Rabbi Eliezer teaches: "The Ark went into exile to Babylonia." He bases his position on a verse from II Chronicles 36:10: "At the turn of the year King Nebuchadnezzar sent and had him brought to Babylon together with the precious vessels of the house of the LORD." This position is also held by Rabbi Simeon bar Yoḥai, who further supports it with a verse from Isaiah (39:6): "Nothing [or no word—that is, the Ten Commandments] shall be left behind, said the LORD." As always in rabbinic discourse, we learn much by looking at the original contexts, since the Rabbis assumed our full knowledge of the Scriptures they quote.

The verse in II Chronicles is found in the final chapter of the Hebrew Bible. It picks up the history of the kings of Israel after the death of King Josiah and the lamentation over his death by the prophet Jeremiah and the people. It describes the precipitous fall into evil by the successors of perhaps the most righteous king in Israel's history, the king who had restored the Temple and reinstated the Passover celebration. Yet this king nonetheless had died on the battlefield meddling in a war that God had warned him not to enter. The chapter's list of evil kings culminates in the destruction of Jerusalem, the sacking of the Temple, and the carrying off of the Ark into exile. However, the chapter—and the Hebrew Bible as a whole—ends on an optimistic note: The King of Persia announces that the people of Israel will be permitted to return and rebuild the Temple, fulfilling the prophecy of Jeremiah. The last word of the Hebrew Bible is *va-ya'al*, "let him go up"—that is, let Israel return to the land; let the exile of the people, and by implication, their God, now end. Not only does Rabbi Eliezer's verse support the view that the Ark was exiled, but, perhaps more important, that it will return.

The context of the verse from Isaiah is similarly fascinating. It occurs at the end of chapter 39. In this chapter King Hezekiah has fallen mortally ill and has been informed by the prophet that he should put his house in order, for he will indeed die before his time. The king, however, prays to God, weeps, and reminds God of his good deeds. In response, God recants, assuring the king fifteen more years of life. Hezekiah recovers, composes a moving prayer of gratitude, and promises to "offer up music all the days of our lives at the House of the LORD"(Isa. 38:20). Immediately following his recovery, the king receives letters and gifts from the king of Babylonia celebrating Hezekiah's recovery. Hezekiah extends his hospitality to the emissaries from Babylonia, displaying for them all of his treasures, his armories, silver, gold, and other precious possessions. He, in fact, reveals to them the location and extent of all his resources. When Isaiah hears of this wanton display, he chastises Hezekiah and prophesies that all that belongs to Hezekiah and the people will one day be carried off to Babylonia; nothing, presumably not even the Ark, will remain.

Chapter 40 begins with the famous prophetic declaration: *Naḥamu naḥamu ami*, "Comfort, oh comfort My people." This is the very chapter of Isaiah that we read in the synagogue on the Shabbat following the Ninth of Av, the anniversary of the destruction of the Temple! Certainly, the Rabbis noted the striking juxtaposition of the quotation in our passage to this consummate statement of comfort. Why does Israel need comfort? For the destruction of the Temple and the exile of the Ark, the exile of God. This magnificent oracle of comfort promises that the Temple will be rebuilt and that Jerusalem will be restored. The Rabbis were also well aware that this prophecy was fulfilled through the agency of the king of Persia, as we learned at the conclusion of our quotation from Chronicles.

Rabbis Eliezer and Simeon bar Yoḥai believe, then, that the issue of whether or not the Ark went into exile is directly related to our belief in the ultimate restoration and redemption of Israel. Both adopt as a kind of orthodoxy that the destruction of Jerusalem was caused by the sinfulness of Israel and that the punishment is a necessary precursor to Israel's restoration, promised at the fullness of time at God's discretion.

Who could dispute this position, sanctified by Scripture and prophet? Apparently, Rabbi Judah bar Ilai. He contends that the Ark is in hiding, basing his contention on the verse in I Kings 8:8 that describes the original installation of the Ark in Solomon's Temple. In the course of his description, he tells us that the poles or staves used for transporting the Ark "projected" so that they could be seen from the sanctuary and that "there they remain to this day." On the basis of this last phrase "to this day," Rabbi Judah contends that the Ark is still in the Temple, buried or otherwise hidden! This view is consistent with similar interpretations in Midrash *Tanḥuma* and is a view quoted by an authority as legitimate and late as Maimonides, who suggests that King Josiah hid the Ark or prepared a hiding place for it anticipating the eventual destruction of the Temple. Similarly, we have traditions that ascribe to Solomon himself the construction of a hiding place for the Ark. What is important to recognize is that the gemara presents two legitimate positions vis-à-vis the disposition of the Ark—hiding and exile—and, thus, two legitimate theologies, a God in exile and a God hidden from God's exiled people.

Our passage now critiques the accuracy of one of the quotations offered in this *baraita*. Apparently Rabbi Simeon bar Yoḥai bases his contention that the Ark went into exile not on the verse previously quoted from Isaiah, but from a verse in Lamentations. In this latter verse, the original biblical context could not be more explicit: Jerusalem and the Temple are being lamented after their destruction. The biblical author writes: "Gone from fair Zion are all that were her glory." Simeon bar Yoḥai identifies this glory as the Ark, not only because of the Ark's central role in Israelite history and theology, but also because of a textual exegesis: The Hebrew word *hadarah* used in Lamentations can mean both "her glory" and "her inner chamber." Simeon bar Yoḥai rests his case: the glory of Israel, her inner chamber—that is, the Ark—is gone into exile.

Armed now with three verses proving that the Ark went into exile, the gemara challenges Rabbi Judah bar Ilai: "What do you say now?" But he holds to his position.

TEXT

What do you say now? He answered: I say that the Ark was hidden in its place, as it is said: "The poles projected," and so on.

INTERPRETATION

Judah bar Ilai bases his opinion on the same verse in I Kings previously used to uphold the opposite view. How is this possible? Let us look more closely at the original biblical context of this verse. In chapter 8, Solomon, after arranging to install the Ark in the Temple, offers an impassioned prayer to God, acknowledging that God does not actually reside in the Temple at all! For if the heavens themselves cannot contain God, certainly a Temple cannot. He prays that this God who transcends space take note of the prayers of Israel. Such a plea is reasonable because prayers offered at the Temple as well as prayers offered in exile are both equally present to an omnipresent God.

Neither Isaiah 39–40 nor the last chapter of II Chronicles—the latter being the source used to support the notion that the Ark was in exile—make mention of the people's prayer as playing any role in God's or the nation's return from exile. On the contrary, such a return is presented as a gift of unearned love, a foreordained fulfillment of a promise, the reward for waiting in faithfulness. However, such is not the theology presented in Solomon's prayer. In that vision, the people must seek God, who has never been contained in a Temple or in a land, who could be anywhere, and who may or may not answer the people's prayers.

The discussion to this point has established the poles of the argument. What follows is a remarkable anthology of biblical verses, mustered to solve the dilemma. We need to remind ourselves, before exploring this list of proof texts, that the result of a talmudic argument is rarely, if ever, the total victory of one side over the other. Quite the contrary, the strength of a talmudic argument—its success, if you will—resides in its ability to awaken in us a sensitivity to the profound tensions of life that must live side by side without resolution. Experience transcends the resolutions of logic; it is, in fact, infinite. The Talmud confronts the intricate problems of human behavior and questions of divine intention knowing that in order to reflect the complexity of truth and the nontotalization of experience, it must create around the tensions that make up both truth and experience a winding rather than a straight path. Along this path we thread our way, guided by a series of biblical quotations on the destruction of Jerusalem, hoping to find our way out to wisdom in the end.

TEXT

Rabba said to Ulla: How does it follow from this? Because it was written: "to this day" (Judg. 1:21). But does the term "to this day" always means "forever"? Is it not written, "The Benjaminites did not dispossess the Jebusite inhabitants of Jerusalem; so the Jebusites have dwelt with the Benjaminites in Jerusalem to this day" (Judg. 1:21). Would you say here, too, that they did not go into exile? Surely it was taught: Rabbi Judah [bar Ilai] said: For fifty-two years no human being passed, as it is said: "For the mountains I take up weeping and a wailing,/ For the pastures in the wilderness, a dirge./ They are laid waste; no man passes through,/ And no sound of the cattle is heard" (Jer. 9:9), and the numerical value of *beheimah* ("cattle") is fifty-two. Furthermore, Rabbi Yose said: "For seven years sulphur and salt prevailed in the land of Israel," and Rabbi Yoḥanan said: "What is the basis of Rabbi Yose's view? He infers it from an analogy of the words 'covenant,' 'covenant.' Here Scripture reads, 'During one week he will make a firm covenant with many' (Dan. 9:27), and in another place it is written, 'They will be told, "Because they forsook the covenant that the LORD, God of their fathers, made with them"'" (Deut. 29:24). He [Rabbi Judah] answered: Here [regarding the Ark] the word "there" ["there they remain to this day," I Kings 8:8] is used; there [in Judges] this expression is not used.

Would you say that wherever the word "there" is used, it implies "forever"? But the following objections can be raised: "And some of them, five hundred of the Simeonites, went to Mount Seir, having for their captains Pelatiah, Neariah, Rephaiah, and Uzziel, sons of Ishi at their head, and they destroyed the last surviving Amalekites, and they live there to this day" (I Chron. 4:42–43). But Sennacherib, King of Assyria, had come up already and confused all the lands, as it is said, "I have erased the borders of peoples and have plundered their treasures" (Isa. 10:13). This is a refutation.

INTERPRETATION

The first quotation, from Judges 1:21, recounts that the tribe of Benjamin failed to drive the Jebusites from Jerusalem at the time of the original conquest of the city. The verse ends by informing us that the Benjaminites and the Jebusites have, therefore, continued to dwell together in Jerusalem "to this day." The text infers from this last phrase a reference to Israel's collective exile, for had the Benjaminites never gone into exile with their fellow countrymen, the verse would have used a phrase such as "forever" or "always." The Talmud goes on to prove, by way of biblical exegesis, that *everyone* in Israel—including the Benjaminites—went into exile together for at least fifty-two years. Quoting Jeremiah 9:9, to which we will return, it numerologically interprets the value of the word *beheimah*, "cattle," to equal fifty-two, concluding that the land was desolate for fifty-two years. Pulling out every exegetical stop to show that "to this day" does not mean "forever," the barrage of evidence continues. We learn that Rabbi Yose said that for seven years sulphur and salt prevailed in the land of Israel, making it uninhabitable. Rabbi Yoḥanan asks, logically enough, on what Rabbi Yose bases his statement. We learn that it is from a verbal analogy between two scriptural appearances of the word "covenant." The two pertinent verses are now introduced, the first from Daniel (9:27) and the second from Deuteronomy (29:24). In each, the word "covenant" appears. In each, the context is a description of the total destruction of the land. The point seems more than amply proved: the Benjaminites could not have avoided the exile; the words "to this day," cannot imply "forever." And the argument, QED: the Ark is not buried beneath the Temple forever, but it, too, has gone into exile.

Following this exchange, Rabbi Judah bar Ilai now attempts to sustain his position on the basis of a very subtle textual point, claiming that, in the verse from Judges, the phrase "to this day" is unmodified. However, the verse he uses from Kings reads, "*there* to this day." Because of this difference, he claims the two verses are not analogous. Thus, although the Benjaminites may well have gone into exile, the Ark did not. The gemara, however, rejects Rabbi Judah's quibble and introduces the final two quotations of our remarkable anthology. The first, from I Chronicles 4:42–43, tells of the destruction of the last Amalekites by the Simeonites, who then occupy their land "there to this day." But the next verse (Isa. 10:13) undercuts its predecessor, for we read there the King of Babylonia's boast that he has scattered all the tribes, not leaving any ancestral boundary undisturbed. In this case, the modifying word "there" has not been able to overturn a textual refutation by another proof text. Rabbi Judah bar Ilai is refuted. And so our passage ends.

The Talmud concludes that the Ark is still in exile, not that it is hidden in the Temple or in the Temple ruins. The mishnah and gemara thus seem to agree: The God of Israel is not hidden; the people have not been abandoned. Rather, God has joined them in their exile in order to comfort them. God's presence in exile gives His people access to Him so that they can seek to expiate their sins; and exile is a punishment of limited duration, in itself an atonement for the nation's collective sins. When their expiation is completed, God and the people both will be restored to their land, their city, and their Temple.

Before accepting this theology at face value, however, we need to ask ourselves two last questions: First, why is Judah bar Ilai's counterposition so threatening that it needed to be thoroughly buried in a storm of biblical proof? To consider this question we will look more closely at the pattern of meaning that emerges from these quotations. Second, assuming that the absence of God is as much a crisis for us now as it was two thousand years ago, which of the two positions of the gemara can we assent to? And are we permitted to choose?

Both questions are related. The Mishnah was compiled after the destruction of the Temple in 70 C.E., after the disastrous Bar Kokhba rebellion of sixty-five years later, and after the catastrophic Hadrianic persecutions that followed in its wake. Yet, it was composed in Israel, not in exile. Presumably, the authors of the Mishnah had attempted to maintain a relationship with God similar to that which had been successfully maintained in Israel throughout the Second Temple period, which preceded its redaction. During the Second Temple period, the priests had performed the rituals of worship as best they could, with the knowledge that the rituals were flawed, since the Ark was missing. During the entire period, the worship had been sustained despite the knowledge that something of God was missing. The *shetiyah*, the foundation stone, had sufficed to represent God's presence. Already during the Second Temple period, the people had a sense of worshiping in a Temple in which God's presence was either hidden or absent. For the framers of the Mishnah who came just after this period and who were themselves not in exile, the question of whether God was hidden or exiled could still not be answered definitively.

In contrast, the Rabbis of the Gemara who followed the mishnaic period were in exile. It made sense for them to emphasize the fact that the Mishnah did not teach that God was hidden in the ruins of the Temple but that God was with the Jewish people in exile. But the ferocity of their response to Rabbi Judah bar Ilai is telling. We can infer that Judah represented a sizable portion of the Jewish people who believed that the God of their ancestors did lie buried in the ruins of their ancestral home. If that were the case, then exile was not a form of atonement shared by God, nor would it necessarily end with the restoration of the national cult when the people's sins had been paid for. Rather, exile was what we might today call an existential state, which originated with the first expulsion in 586 B.C.E. No amount of ceremony in the Second Temple could mask this one crucial fact: there was no Ark at the center. Rabbi Judah's position must certainly have struck a chord to have elicited such a strong response. It therefore behooves us to take his position seriously. Let us now look more closely at the pattern of argument embodied in the anthology of biblical quotations in our text.

Ten biblical quotations appear in this short passage. Nine are used to support the idea that the Ark is in exile; one, to support the idea that it is hidden. Yet, in eight of these nine verses, the biblical context betrays a trace of uncertainty that seems to legitimize the position of Rabbi Judah bar Ilai even as his opponents struggle to refute him.

The first verse quoted in this series, from II Chronicles, is quite clear: Exiling the people was God's way of re-establishing the sacred economy that Israel's sins had upset: "as long as it lay desolate it kept sabbath, till seventy years were completed" (II Chron. 36:21). The restoration that ends the exile comes only when the sabbatical years unobserved by Israel have been paid back. Thus, exile is not an existential state but a temporary period to allow for expiation. In order for that expiation to be effected, God must accompany Israel into exile. However, this verse is immediately undercut by Isaiah 39:6 and its context leading into Isaiah 40. For, although these chapters speak of the exile, they intimate that nothing will be left. They also emphasize the universal activity of God, divine providence, and they question the possibility that human beings can fathom God's actions. The Talmud here establishes its telltale pattern in this anthology of proof texts: a posture of equivocation. On the one hand, Israel must believe in a God who is with them in exile, an experience that will serve as an expiation. Yet, at the same time, they also must wrestle with their experience of trauma and dislocation caused by this very God and their feeling of abandonment implied by the symbol of a hidden God.

This pattern becomes more pronounced with the next pair of verses (if we exclude Rabbi Judah's verse from I Kings). In Lamentations we read of the utter hopelessness of Israel: Jerusalem has no comforter! In contradistinction to Isaiah, Lamentations paints a picture of trauma that no theology can mollify. The only reasonable response is grief. And the chapter in Judges cited after this verse in our text implies that from its earliest years Jerusalem was not fully conquerable by Israel and not solely inhabited by Israel. Thus, the sense that exile represents abandonment by God grows, even while, as we showed above, the opposite case is being constructed by a surface use of these verses without their larger context.

To this picture Jeremiah adds a new and essential piece of information: God's wrath will not be aimed at Israel alone. Whereas Israel is uncircumcised in the heart, the people of other nations are physically uncircumcised. Both are, therefore, uncovenanted! And God will punish the uncovenanted. But then, Israel cannot think of God as being with them in exile. For, if all peoples are uncovenanted, all are equally subject to the punishment of exile. Is the whole world, then, a place of exile? If so, how can we say whether God is present or absent? Again we see that ambivalence, and—what is more important—that the "problem" of God's absence has been linked to the concept of a covenant, a concept taken up directly in the next pair of verses.

The selections from the Books of Daniel and Deuteronomy are crucial and form the heart of our passage. In Chapter 9 of Daniel, the future is foretold in a vision in answer to Daniel's prayer that the Temple be restored. Echoes of some of our other passages abound. Verse 9:17, for example, recalls Solomon's prayer from Kings. Verse 18 recalls Hezekiah's prayer in Isaiah. The entire chapter is an elucidation of the prophecy of Jeremiah, and the word "covenant" is used twice in the chapter. At the beginning of the chapter, Daniel refers to the covenant of God's mercy extended to those who keep God's commandments. We also learn, in verse 27, that after the Temple is restored, it will be destroyed again. A foreign king will then make a covenant with the people to rebuild the Temple, but he will not keep his promise, and the Temple will be utterly destroyed. This vision of the Second Temple's annihilation is not like Isaiah's or Jeremiah's visions of the First Temple's ruin. This is utter destruction, not mere exile.

The Talmud links this vision in Daniel to the covenant mentioned in Deuteronomy 29:24, where the context is similar. The Torah foretells that Israel will forsake its covenant with God, who will then root them out of their land: "and cast them into another land, *as it is this day*," using a phrase almost identical to the one that the gemara has been debating. These verses from Daniel and Deuteronomy are clearly different from the earlier verses. Although Daniel foresees the restoration of Jerusalem as prophesied by Jeremiah and Isaiah, he sees that restoration as flawed and as followed by an even more horrible destruction, the very destruction actually facing the Rabbis. The context of Daniel and Deuteronomy both seem to place the blame for this destruction on the people's sinfulness and to suggest that the destruction itself is not a sufficient expiation. Prayer and a recommitment to the covenant are required.

Immediately following these prophecies in Deuteronomy, we read a remarkable verse: "Concealed [or "secret"] acts concern the LORD our God; but with overt acts it is for us and our children *[for]ever* to apply all the provisions of this Teaching" (Deut. 29:28). In the development of our interpretation, this verse adds a new and powerful suggestion: That which is hidden, the secrets and mysteries of God's place, of ways of understanding and or manipulating God, should not concern us. We should worry less about where God is and more about where we are; worry less about how we can use God's place for our benefit and worry more about sustaining the ancient covenant. Thus, a third pole in the gemara's argument emerges, one that changes the very question we are asking.

In that light, we return to Chronicles and Isaiah, where we began. In Chronicles, we read of the original conquest of the land, the difficult, dangerous, often incomplete work of establishing a nation. In Isaiah, we read that ultimately it is God alone who disposes land. How vain are those who boast that they are responsible for their own success: "Does an ax boast over him who hews with it?" (Isa. 10:15). Then, after reading the development of this metaphor: "Lo! The Sovereign LORD of Hosts/ Will hew off the tree-crowns with an ax" (Isa. 10:33), we come to the opening verses of Chapter 11: "But a shoot shall grow out of the stump of Jesse,/ A twig shall sprout from his stock./ The spirit of the LORD shall alight upon him,/ A spirit of wisdom and insight,/ A spirit of counsel and valor,/ A spirit of devotion and reverence for the LORD" (Isa. 11:1–2). Perhaps it is not for us to ascertain whether God is in hiding or in exile. Such a question can only be answered by the Davidic Messiah anticipated by this verse. In the meantime, our time should be spent hastening the coming of that Messiah by re-establishing our commitment to the covenant: by showing concern for the widow, orphan, and stranger; love of neighbor and of God; for in these acts we will surely find God, whether hidden or exiled.

It remains for us to return to our original question: How do we seek atonement without a Temple? If God is absent, is it because God is in exile or hiding? These questions confront post-Holocaust Jews as much as post–70 C.E. Jews. In the course of debating whether the Ark was hidden or went into exile, the gemara has suggested how we can live with the ambivalence that must accompany any attempt to resolve this argument. To do so, we must believe that God is with us in exile, for without the comfort of such a belief, the darkness of existential exile would be too much to bear. The mishnah adopts this faith, but with some hesitancy. The gemara removes this hesitancy by marshaling a host of traditional prophecies to support it. Ironically, these "prophecies" all look backward rather than to the future! Jeremiah and Isaiah, Chronicles and Lamentations predict, report, and mourn the First Temple's destruction and look forward to its restoration. Only Daniel predicted the destruction of the Second Temple. His vision of the future was different from the others'. To Daniel, restoration does not require the expiation of exile. Rather, his vision demands that Israel reaffirm its original covenant.

Both the mishnah and gemara suggest that the problem facing survivors of the Roman conquest had previously faced survivors of the Babylonian exile six centuries before. For the Second Temple, when it was restored after the return from Babylonia, never had an Ark. Whether hidden or still in exile, it was absent. In the Second Temple the High Priest, lacking the Ark, had to rest his fire pan on the "foundation stone." Thus, the restoration is never complete. But the search for God, the re-enactment of the covenant, in effect, completes the restoration. After the destruction of the Second Temple only the Messiah, as described by Isaiah, could effect restoration. That restoration depends on the people's success at bringing the Messiah through re-enacting the covenant. After the Temple's destruction, an aspect of God forever lay hidden, forever was in exile. If that was the case then, what can we say now?

For us, even the hope of a Messiah is difficult to maintain. We do not debate so much whether God is hidden or in exile, but, rather, whether God even remains in the world at all. In the gemara's notion of reaffirming the covenant, we take the first steps toward restoring our faith. The idea of covenant cannot be accidental in the anthology of verses we have been exploring. The word is simply too powerful and too persistent. And though the covenant is ostensibly contracted between God and Israel, we find most of its terms anchored in human relationship. If we are to locate God in our own world and time, we will need to recognize, as the gemara does, that exile and hiddenness are synonymous. In choosing verses concerning the covenant, the gemara is suggesting that we read the story of the missing Ark as a parable: When human beings are alienated from each other, the Ark is in exile; when the image of God cannot be discerned in the human face, the Ark is in hiding. And the Foundation Stone upon which we now appeal for atonement is the very foundation of the covenant itself: "Love your fellow as yourself" (Lev. 19:18); "The stranger who resides with you shall be to you as one of your citizens; you shall love him as yourself, for you were strangers in the land of Egypt" (Lev. 19:34); "you shall be holy, for I, the LORD your God, am holy" (Lev. 19:2).

CONSTRUCTING THE GATEWAY TO HEAVEN

Sukkah 44b–45a

TEXT

Mishnah

How did they carry out the precept of the willow branch? There was a place below Jerusalem called *Motza*. They went down there and gathered young willow branches and then came and fixed them at the sides of the altar so that their tops bent over the altar; they then sounded a *teki'ah* [long blast], a *teru'ah* [tremulous blast], and again a *teki'ah*. Every day they went round the altar once, saying, "We beseech You, O Lord, please save, we beseech You, O Lord, let us please prosper." Rabbi Judah said, [they were saying], *"Ani vaho*, save now." But on that day they went around the altar seven times. When they departed, what did they say? "Yours, O altar, is the beauty! Yours, O altar, is the beauty!" Rabbi Eliezer said, [They were saying,] "To the Lord and to You, O altar, to the Lord and to You, O altar."

As was its performance on a weekday, so was its performance on the Sabbath, save that they gathered them on the eve [of the

Sabbath] and placed them in golden basins that they might not become mildewed. Rabbi Yoḥanan ben Beroka said, they used to bring palm twigs and beat them on the ground at the sides of the altar, and that day was called "[the day of] the beating of the palm twigs." They used to take their *lulavim* [branches of palms, willows, and myrtles bound together] from the hands of the children and eat their *etrogim* [citrons].

Gemara

It was taught, it was the place called Kolonia. Then why does our *Tanna* call it *Motza* [exempt]? Since it was exempt from the king's tax, he calls it *Motza*.

"And then came and fixed them at the sides of," and so on. A *Tanna* taught, They were large and long and eleven cubits high, so that they might bend over the altar one cubit. Meremar, citing Mar Zutra, observed, Deduce from this that they were laid upon the base [of the altar], for if you were to assume that they were placed on the ground, consider this: It rose up one cubit and drew in one cubit, and this formed the base. It then rose up five cubits and drew in one cubit, and this formed the circuit; it [then] rose up three cubits, and this was the place of the horns. Now how could they bend over the altar? Consequently, it may be deduced from this that they were laid on the base. This is conclusive. Rabbi Abbahu said, "What is its Scriptural proof?" Since it is said, "Bind the festival offering to the horns of the altar with cords"(Pss. 118:27).

Rabbi Abbahu, citing Rabbi Eleazar, stated: Whoever takes the *lulav* with its bindings and the willow branch with its wreathing is regarded by Scripture as though he had built an altar and offered on it a sacrifice, for it is said, "Bind the festival offering to the horns of the altar with cords"(Pss. 118:27). Rabbi Yirmeyah, citing Rabbi Simeon bar Yoḥai, and Rabbi Yoḥanan, citing Rabbi Simeon of Mahoz, who had it from Rabbi Yoḥanan of Makkut, stated: Whoever makes an addition to the festival by eating and drinking is regarded by Scripture as though he had built an altar and offered on it a sacrifice, for it is said, "Bind the festival offering to the horns of the altar with cords"(Pss. 118:27).

Hezekiah, citing Rabbi Yirmeyah, who had it from Rabbi Simeon bar Yoḥai, stated: In the case of all commandments, one does not fulfill one's obligation unless [the objects involved] are in the same condition as when they grow, for it is said: "Acacia wood upright" (Exod. 26:15). So it was also taught, "Acacia wood upright" implies that they should stand in the manner of their growth." Another interpretation: "upright" implies that they held their [gold] overlaying. Another interpretation of "upright": Lest you may say, "Their hope is lost, their expectation is frustrated," Scripture expressly states, "Acacia wood upright," implying that they will stand forever and to all eternity.

Hezekiah further stated in the name of Rabbi Yirmeyah, who said it in the name of Rabbi Simeon bar Yoḥai: I am able to exempt the whole world from judgment from the day that I was born until now, and were Eliezer, my son, to be with me [we could exempt it] from the day of the creation of the world to the present time, and were Yotam the son of Uzziah with us, [we could exempt it] from the creation of the world to its final end.

Hezekiah further stated in the name of Rabbi Yirmeyah, who said it in the name of Rabbi Simeon bar Yoḥai, I have seen the sons of heaven and they are but few. If there be a thousand, I and my son are among them; if a hundred, I and my son are among them; and if only two, they are I and my son.

Are they then so few? Did not Raba in fact state: The row [of righteous men immediately] before the Holy One, blessed be He, consists of eighteen thousand, for it is said, "Its circumference [shall be] eighteen thousand [cubits]"(Ezek. 48:35)? This is no difficulty: The former number refers to those who see Him through a bright speculum; the latter, to those who see Him through a dim one. But are those who see Him through a bright speculum so few? Did not Abbaye in fact state: The world never has fewer than thirty-six righteous men who are vouchsafed a sight of the *Shekhinah* every day, for it is said, "Happy are all who wait for Him *(lo)*(Isa. 30:18) and the numerical value of *(lo)* is thirty-six? There is no difficulty: The latter number refers to those who may enter [the Presence] with permission; the former, to those who may enter without permission.

INTERPRETATION

The building of a *sukkah* is a consummate act of worship. Building a *sukkah* recapitulates the worship of the Jewish people in the wilderness—namely, the construction of the Tabernacle. The connection between the *sukkah* and the Tabernacle and the connection between the Tabernacle or

Temple in this world and its ideal in the next are not uncommon themes in our literature. In this passage, the gemara explores these connections and the tradition's ultimate construction project—neither *sukkah*, nor Tabernacle, nor Temple—but the construction of meaning.

We begin with the mishnah. It describes the ritual of the willow branch, a ritual associated with the festival of Sukkot but not described in the Torah or fully captured by the rituals associated with Sukkot in post-Temple times. The Torah simply requires that the willow be taken, together with the palm, the myrtle, and the citron *(etrog)*, and waved before God. A wave offering was not unusual among the various Temple offerings. The mishnah describes the evolution of this ritual from its sparse biblical beginnings to later practice.

Returning to the mishnah, we read that the precept of the willow mentioned in the Torah was fulfilled in the Temple as follows. First, the willows were gathered in a rural suburb below Jerusalem called *Motza*. This was actually a place called Kolonia but referred to as *Motza*—"exempt"—presumably because it was exempt from the king's taxes. These collected willows were fixed at the sides of the altar so that they bent over the altar. Each day the shofar would be blown (the same penitential notes that are blown during the Rosh Hashanah liturgy), while the priests marched around the altar saying, "We beseech You, O Lord, save now. We beseech You, O Lord, let us please prosper." But on the day of the ritual of the willow they went around the altar seven times saying: "Yours, O altar, is the beauty! Yours, O altar, is the beauty!" According to Rabbi Eliezer, who wants to avoid any suspicion of pagan worship, they would not have invoked the altar without also invoking God; they said "To You, Lord, and to you, O altar, to the Lord and to you, O altar." The mishnah concludes by describing the differences between weekdays and Shabbat, as well as the concluding acts of the festival: the beating of the palms and the eating of the *etrog*.

We have already referred to the explanation of the term *Motza* in the first paragraph in our passage of the gemara. The longer second paragraph teaches us that the willows in question were inserted on the base of the altar, not on the ground. We learn this through a comparison between the measurements of the altar and the measurements of the willows. This proof is considered conclusive, but a scriptural proof text is also provided: "Bind the festival offerings to the horns of the altar with cords" (Pss. 118:27). The verse, which Rabbi Abbahu himself had initially quoted as proof that the willows were fixed in the base of the altar, is now interpreted in a dramatically different way: "Whosoever takes the

lulav with its binding and the willow branch with its wreathing is regarded by Scripture as though he had built an altar and offered thereon a
sacrifice." This verse is now applied, not to the time of the Temple, but to
the post-Temple reality, in which people asked how they could achieve
the access to God that they once had through the Temple; how they could
prepare their environment for seeking redemption; how they could construct a new gateway to heaven. Whoever does what Rabbi Abbahu rec-
ommends is regarded as having done what literally cannot be done!

From this point, our passage moves quickly through a series of exegeses informing us, first, of other such imaginary acts of building the
altar and offering sacrifices; second, of the purpose of offering sacrifices;
and third, of the goal of offering sacrifices, presented in a heavenly vision. However, before we allow ourselves to be carried along by these
exegeses, we must stop and look more closely at their primary source
and the underlying text for this discussion, Psalm 118.

Psalm 118 is the last of a series of psalms—113 through part of 118—
that are included in the *Hallel* liturgy. These are psalms of praise and
thanksgiving sung on festivals. The language of Psalm 118 points to its
origin as a psalm of rededication of the Temple at the Sukkot celebration, perhaps after the Maccabean victory. Others connect its composi-
tion with the celebration of Sukkot described in the Book of Nehemiah
(8:14). Either way, its strong and ancient connection with Sukkot and the
Temple is undisputed. It is a psalm that narrates a road from despair to
redemption. It begins with a refrain expressing faith in God's mercy and
a special reminder of the priesthood's faith in God's mercy: "Let the
house of Aaron declare,/ 'His steadfast love is eternal'" (Pss. 118:3).

It continues by describing the depths of despair from which the
psalmist heard the saving answer of God's mercy. It catalogues in detail
the dangers that surrounded the speaker and the strength of God to redeem him. Its narrative leads up the steps of the Temple to the very
gates. "The stone that the builders rejected"—that is, the Temple—"is
become the chief cornerstone" (Pss. 118:22). Thus, "The LORD is God;/
He has given us light;/ Bind the festival offering to the horns of the altar
with cords" (Pss. 118:27). But in Rabbi Abbahu's time and our own time,
there is no Temple, and there can be no altar! There is no gate! The
psalm silently returns us to the question of our passage in the gemara,
the question of building an altar. The answer of Rabbi Abbahu is set in
the context of Psalm 118. The festival boughs, the procession with those
boughs, and the faith in God's mercy, taken together, are an "as if" ritual. It is "as if" we had built an altar.

However, the question of the Temple's disappearance is not and cannot be answered on the basis of even the most daring act of religious imagination. Our ability to construe our acts as having the power to rebuild the altar does not mean that they accomplish this, nor does it account for the traumas that may have destroyed our faith in redemption in the first place. These are the questions the gemara takes up after enumerating the various acts of ritual that might contribute to this imaginary rebuilding project.

The more difficult questions we have suggested are introduced by Hezekiah in the name of Rabbi Yirmeyah, who introduces Rabbi Simeon bar Yoḥai to the discussion. This is the Rabbi Simeon bar Yoḥai who is reported to have spent thirteen years in a cave with his son, Eliezer, hiding from Roman persecution and suffering privation. On the basis of this suffering, Rabbi Simeon bar Yoḥai declares that for the entire span of his life the world is exempt from judgment. That is, his suffering is a sufficient expiation for the sinfulness of the world. Moreover, claims Rabbi Simeon, in the course of his troubles he has had a vision of those who have been righteous enough to stand before the throne of God. His own and his son's suffering guarantee that they will stand before that throne, even if no one else be deemed righteous enough to stand with them.

These statements of Rabbi Simeon bar Yoḥai exacerbate the tension that this passage now attempts to confront through an essential discussion in fundamental theology. Psalm 118 provides the metaphor within which this discussion takes place. We are searching, if you will, for the gateway to heaven. Rabbi Simeon has glimpsed that gateway from the depths of his suffering, but his glimpse is fleeting and leaves him with an unclear vision. Are there a thousand, a hundred, or merely two, standing before the throne? Is heaven for the few or the many? In a world without an altar, can redemption be sought with songs of joy, or only through suffering, or not at all? Is redemption a free gift of God's grace, or must it be sought out?

The gemara assumes that even if Rabbi Simeon bar Yoḥai saw one thousand souls standing before the throne, this is a very small number, relatively speaking. To counter this conclusion, the gemara introduces a verse from Ezekiel, understood as describing the scene before the throne: "Its circumference [shall be] eighteen thousand [cubits]." The gemara attempts to harmonize the thousand of Rabbi Simeon with the eighteen thousand of Ezekiel by asserting that they refer to two different groups—the many who will have a hazy view of the throne from afar and the few who will have a clear view from close by. Rabbi Simeon has suggested that the number of souls close by the throne might number only two. Yet Abbaye's account indicates that there are a minimum of thirty-six men who see God clearly every day, based on a verse in Isaiah (30:18), "Happy are all who wait for Him [*lo*]." The numerical value of the Hebrew world *lo* is 36. This discrepancy, too, is harmonized by the gemara. These thirty-six enter the throne room of God by permission; Rabbi Simeon bar Yoḥai and his son enter without permission.

We must remember that three biblical verses are being discussed in this passage: verses from Psalm 118, Ezekiel, and Isaiah. The context of our discussion is the power of the altar to effect redemption and the transference of this power to the festival procession and other acts of imaginary altar-building as implied by the exegesis of Psalm 118. In this context, the two prophetic verses can be understood as pertinent to the question of how we successfully build imaginary altars. According to Rabbi Simeon, only suffering effects redemption in the post-Temple world. However, the verses from Ezekiel and Isaiah are used by the gemara to critique Rabbi Simeon's position. No one can deny that suffering is a part of Israel's experience, as understood both by Ezekiel and Isaiah. But the contexts of both selected verses provides a different slant on the place of Israel's suffering.

The verse from Ezekiel (48:35) is the final one of the book. Though not quoted in its entirety (a standard practice since the Talmud assumed of its readers an encyclopedic knowledge of Scripture), the final, and most important, words of the verse are "and the name of the city from that day on shall be 'The LORD Is There.'" This verse comes at the end of the lengthy third segment of the Book of Ezekiel, which describes in minute detail the Jerusalem and Temple of the future! It is the most complete imagined rebuilding of the Temple known to Judaism, founded on a vision of hope vouchsafed to the prophet and through the prophet to the people. It describes an end to exile because God faithfully remembers the people Israel and the covenant. Israel's suffering is transformed into the first stage of a messianic cataclysm, the War of Gog and Magog, which, in turn, will precede a universal redemption for the world. This redemption is precipitated by the suffering of the whole people; through that suffering, redemption becomes available to them. Rabbi Simeon's suffering brings only him closer to the divine throne, but all Israel has certainly suffered enough to warrant at least a dim view of the throne.

The verse from the Book of Isaiah is found in the context of a prophecy against Israel's making foreign alliances, instead of depending entirely on God for support. Verse 30:15, for example, reads: "You shall triumph by stillness and quiet; Your victory shall come about/ Through calm and confidence. . . ." Verse 30:18 in its entirety reads: "Truly the LORD is waiting to show you grace,/ Truly, He will arise to pardon you./ For the LORD is a God of justice;/ Happy are all who wait for Him" (*lo* = 36). The verse from Ezekiel qualified Rabbi Simeon's position by teaching that redemption is available to all Israel, not only to a sufferer like Rabbi Simeon, through building an imaginary Temple. The verse from Isaiah shifts the emphasis from personal suffering as the road to redemption to patient trust in God as the road to redemption. But not to take it into our own hands to effect redemption but rather to wait for God seems to challenge not only Rabbi Simeon, but Ezekiel too. Is it possible to act "as if" we could find an alternative to the Temple? The Rabbis may be using the verse from Isaiah to consider the possibility that we cannot.

In doing so, an alternative possibility is introduced which requires a new reading of the entire argument up to this point. This alternative may well be considered the goal toward which the discussion has been proceeding. It is the introduction of the legend of the thirty-six righteous souls upon whom depends the existence of the world.

This idea, embellished throughout later Jewish history, that there are thirty-six righteous souls for whose sake the world is not destroyed, has its origin in our passage. It is also cited in three parallel passages, one in Tractate *Ḥullin* and two in Midrash *Genesis Rabbah*. The legend can be approached from two directions. On the one hand it indicates the general unworthiness of the world to survive; we should not be surprised that the world seems constantly on the brink of destruction. On the other hand, it indicates the patience and compassion of God. Given the myriad human beings on the planet, only thirty-six are required to be righteous for the world to continue. More important, the Talmud is asserting that suffering of itself does not effect redemption (in the form of God's compassion); rather righteousness does.

The version of this story that appears in Tractate *Ḥullin* is the form of an exegeses of a verse in Hosea (3:2): "Then I hired her (*va-ekreha*) for fifteen shekels of silver, a *homer* of barley, a *letech* of barley." The gemara continues:

> Said Rabbi Yoḥanan in the name of Rabbi Simeon ben Yehotzadak, the word *kirah* must mean "buying," for so it is written, "In my

grave which I bought *[kariti]* for me" (Gen. 50:5). "For fifteen": that is, the fifteenth of Nisan, when Israel was redeemed out of Egypt. "Shekels of silver": these are the righteous, for so it is written: "He took his bag of money with him" (Prov. 7:20). "And a *homer* of barley and a *letech* of barley": these are the forty-five righteous men on account of whom the world continues to exist.

Thus, in this version of the story, the number of righteous is different, and their role in the world is a specific continuation of the process of redemption begun in Egypt with the Exodus! The continuation of the world is an extension of redemption.

In *Genesis Rabbah* the story appears again, in a version closer to the story in our passage.

It is taught by Rabbi Hezekiah in the name of Rabbi Yirmeyah that Rabbi Simeon bar Yoḥai said: The world possesses not fewer than thirty men as righteous as Abraham. If there are thirty, my son and I are two of them; if five, my son and I are two of them; if two, they are my son and I; if there is but one, it is I.

This time Rabbi Simeon's statements are attached to the verse in Genesis, "God further said, 'This is the sign that I set for the covenant between Me and you . . . for all ages to come'" (Gen. 9:12). Thus, the world's continuity is both an extension of redemption and the fulfillment of the covenant.

The story appears again in *Genesis Rabbah,* this time in connection with the story of the destruction of Sodom and Abraham's argument with God. God says: "Shall I hide from Abraham what I am about to do, since Abraham is to become *[hayo yihyeh]* a great and populous nation, and all the nations of the earth are to bless themselves by him? For I have singled him out, that he may instruct his children and his posterity to keep the way of the LORD by doing what is just and right, in order that the LORD may bring about for Abraham what He has promised him" (Gen. 18:17–19). Rabbi Tanḥum said in the name of Rabbi Hus Ela in Rabbi Berekhya's name: He informed him that the world must never contain less than thirty righteous men like Abraham. Rabbi Yudan and Rabbi Ala in Rabbi Alexandri's name deduced it from this verse: "since Abraham is to become"—*hayo yihyeh*—*yud* is ten; *heh,* five; *yud,* ten; and *heh,* five.

Thus, in our final example, the thirty righteous men are defined in the context of Abraham's righteousness, the righteousness of arguing with God to save the lives of the possible good people left in Sodom!

The challenge in our gemara to Rabbi Simeon bar Yoḥai's claim to redemption on the basis of suffering is from a counter claim that the world is sustained not by suffering but by acts of moral strength. This righteousness is patterned after Abraham's fighting for the threatened and oppressed. It is in our passage that the number reaches thirty-six: "Happy are all who wait for Him" (lo = 36). Our passage also endeavors to assess and, I think, judge, the relative merits of these two models of effecting redemption: suffering versus acts of moral strength.

We note first that the legend of the thirty-six righteous men is not quoted in the version attributed to Rabbi Simeon bar Yoḥai but, rather, in direct opposition to the position of Rabbi Simeon. And the gemara states that there is no problem between them: they simply apply to different situations. Rabbi Simeon's contention that his suffering earned him redemption is redemption achieved without permission, while the redemption achieved by virtue of the thirty-six righteous men was achieved with permission. We have only to understand the meaning of these phrases, "with permission" and "without permission," to understand our passage's idea of how to replace the altar and effect redemption.

Both paths to redemption are possible; both are, perhaps, necessary. One who suffers does not need permission to enter the heavenly circle and gain redemption. For such a person, redemption is automatic. Human suffering does not require any judgment on the part of God— sufferers ascend. For those who do not suffer, who want to achieve redemption apart from suffering, the primary road is by modeling oneself on Abraham and fighting against suffering. These are the two options that our passage leaves for building an altar of the imagination. We either take on suffering for the world, or fight for others not to suffer. There must be at least thirty-six righteous souls in the world, fighting against the oppression of others.

It is now clear how it is possible to build an altar, construct a Temple, effect redemption, all without an actual Temple in Jerusalem: either by undergoing suffering or by alleviating it. And in the sukkah we open ourselves to both possibilities. We experience our insignificance in the face of the elements; and we invite the hungry, the homeless, and the disenfranchised to join us in our home, to which the door is never shut. For some of us the very act of building the sukkah can be an act of suffering endured. It is an act loved even more in light of the significance of its meaning: constructing a gateway to heaven through which the righteous approach the Divine Presence.

WHAT IS HANUKKAH?

Shabbat 21a–22a

TEXT

Rabbi Ḥuna said: With regard to the wicks and oils of which the Sages said, "One must not light with them on the Sabbath," one may not light with them on Hanukkah, either on the Sabbath or on weekdays. Raba observed, What is Rabbi Ḥuna's reason? He holds that if it [the Hanukkah lamp] goes out, one must attend to it, and one may make use of its light. Rabbi Ḥisda maintained: One may light with them on weekdays, but not on the Sabbath. He holds that if it goes out, it does *not* require attention, and one may make use of its light.

Rabbi Zera said in Rabbi Mattena's name—others state, Rabbi Zera said in Rav's name: Regarding the wicks and oils which the Sages said, One must not light with them on the Sabbath, one may light with them on Hanukkah, either on weekdays or on the Sabbath. Said Rabbi Yirmeyah, What is Rav's reason? He holds, If it goes out, it does *not* require attention, and one may *not* make use of its light.

The Rabbis stated this before Abbaye in Rabbi Yirmeyah's name, but he did not accept it. [But] when Rabin came, the Rabbis stated it before Abbaye in Rabbi Yoḥanan's name, whereupon he accepted it. Had I, he observed, merited the great fortune, I would have learned this teaching originally. But he learned it [now]? The difference is in respect of the studies of one's youth.

INTERPRETATION

How do you feel on the birthday of a loved one not long dead? Is it a day of celebration or of mourning? Our celebration of Hanukkah, long misunderstood, is bound up with the answer to this question. In recent years we have debated: Is Hanukkah a major holiday or a minor one? Should it be emphasized or de-emphasized vis-à-vis Christmas? Does it celebrate the Maccabean victory over the Greco-Syrians or the victory of Jewish pietists over assimilationists? And finally, what, if any, is the relationship between the miracle of the Maccabean victory and the miracle of the oil? All of these contemporary questions miss the fundamental question that faced the first-, second-, and third-century Rabbis, who were charged with salvaging from Jewish history a reason for persisting in the face of tragedy. In this discussion, Hanukkah plays an important role.

In the midst of a discussion in Tractate *Shabbat* concerning the fitness of various types of oils and wicks for use as Sabbath lights, Hanukkah is suddenly brought in. At first glance, the logic is impeccable: We've been talking about lighting lights, and the most singular characteristic of Hanukkah is the lighting of lights. Yet it ought to shock us! Hanukkah is not mentioned in the mishnah of Shabbat or in any other mishnah! Hanukkah is not mentioned in any authoritative book of the Bible (the Rabbis having chosen to omit the Book of the Maccabees from the canon)! How do we know about it? What is it? What does it commemorate? How is it observed? None of these questions precede the sudden introduction of a minor detail of its observance.

In this light, the nonchalant segue from Shabbat to Hanukkah cannot be taken for granted. When Rabbi Ḥuna states categorically, "With regard to the wicks and oils of which the Sages said, 'One must not light with them on the Sabbath,' one may not light with them on Hanukkah, either on the Sabbath or on weekdays," he is conveying the sanction of the Sages for the observance of Hanukkah. Moreover, he thereby conveys Hanukkah's importance by comparing it with Shabbat. This likeness is not, however, a foregone conclusion. The silence about Hanukkah up until this point in the chain of rabbinic tradition must reflect the fact that the Rabbis had a significant problem with observing Hanukkah, which is here being subtly challenged.

Raba begins to unpack Rabbi Ḥuna's understanding of the tradition. According to Raba, Rabbi Ḥuna holds that the equivalence of Shabbat and Hanukkah can be proved by two relevant halakhic traditions: first, if the Hanukkah lights go out, they must be rekindled, and second, their light *may* be used for reading. Hence, they require fine oil of the quality of Shabbat, though not, as we shall see, for the same reason. On Shabbat the sacral lights may *not* be rekindled *nor* used for reading. Furthermore, in honor of the day and in order that the lights not go out or burn with a distasteful odor, fine oil and wicks that prolong and enhance the burning are required. So, according to Rabbi Ḥuna, Hanukkah and Shabbat are alike in that fine oil and wicks are used for both, but for different reasons.

By contrast, Raba tells us, "Rabbi Ḥisda maintained: One may light with them [the oils and wicks prohibited on Shabbat] on weekdays [during Hanukkah], but not on the Sabbath. He holds that if it [the Hanukkah lamp] goes out, it does not require attention [that is, does not need to be rekindled], and one may make use of its light." Rabbi Ḥisda's position would seem to indicate that only when Hanukkah falls on Shabbat do the two holidays have anything in common, and only because of the honor of Shabbat do we accord Hanukkah any religious significance. We shall return to this position in a moment.

Before hearing the third ruling, that of Rav, we must note two facts—one in the text, one hovering above it. The tradition reported in Rav's name is not reported "cleanly." The fact that the Talmud frequently reports traditions in which the chain of oral tradition is not clear (here either Rabbi Zera quoting Rabbi Mattena or Rabbi Zera quoting Rav) indicates the tradition's willingness to acknowledge the unreliability in its own development. The note of uncertainty thus introduced should be read as part of the discussion, not as a "mere" or "minor" confusion. The difference between the purported speakers of this particular tradition is also important. Rabbi Mattena is a minor *amoraic* authority, whereas Rav is a major rabbinic figure, the first of the *Amoraim* and last of the *Tannaim.* The weight of the difference between the two must be relevant. Moreover, immediately after Rav's statement, the confusion continues, for Abbaye, Rav's partner and equal to him in authority, changes his mind on the issue, admitting that he had not learned a tradition properly as a youth. We will investigate the exposition of this confusion as we proceed through the text.

Either Rabbi Mattena or Rav said: "Regarding the wicks and oils of which the Sages said, 'One must not light with them on the Sabbath,' one may light therewith on Hanukkah, either on weekdays *or* on the Sabbath. Said Rabbi Yirmeyah, What is Rav's reason? He holds, If it goes out it does not require attention and one may *not* make use of its light."

We now have before us the three possible positions. Rabbi Ḥuna endorses the sanctity of Hanukkah, which he holds is comparable to that of Shabbat, but not as restrictive. Rabbi Ḥisda challenges that Hanukkah has no sanctity. Finally Rav, or Rabbi Mattena, maintains that Hanukkah has no intrinsic sanctity but is nevertheless celebrated as if it did. These positions are deduced by surveying the four categories set up in the gemara:

1. Whether Shabbat-quality oil and wicks must be used.
2. Whether this use falls on Shabbat or on Shabbat and weekdays.
3. Whether the Hanukkah lights must be rekindled if they go out.
4. Whether one may make use of the lights.

The reason given for Rav's position is supplied by Rabbi Yirmeyah. When this rationale was reported to Abbaye, he did not accept it. The gemara does not initially explain Abbaye's reason for rejecting Rabbi Yirmeyah's explanation of Rav's ruling. I suggest that he rejects this reasoning precisely because it is contradictory. If the lamp does not require attention, if only on the Sabbath do we treat it with any of the honor due the Sabbath lamp, then it does not make sense to restrict the use which may be made of the lamp! Perhaps, however, it is in the very nature of this festival to be contradictory. What if one were trying to convey that Hanukkah is a festival that is not on the sacred calendar but is nevertheless observed, and that, once observed, takes on a level of popular sanctity? Under those circumstances, perhaps there is indeed room for contradictory reading.

When Abbaye is confronted with the same explanation of Rav's ruling a second time, this time in the name of Rabbi Yoḥanan, he recants, ostensibly because Rabbi Yoḥanan is a greater authority than Rabbi Yirmeyah. However, Abbaye simply tells us, "Had I merited great fortune I would have learned this teaching originally." The "narrator" of the gemara further informs us that this is because one's youthful studies are better. There may well be much truth in this statement, but Abbaye was no amateur scholar. He was a master of his generation. Is his confusion over the status of Hanukkah merely the result of his not having learned well enough in his youth? This could hardly be the case.

The reference to youth in the context of Hanukkah feels more than coincidental. Is it not a festival of particular importance to children?

Would it not have been an observance clung to by parents on account of children regardless of its having been left out of the official calendar? Who could resist the glow of the lights in winter's darkness? The remembrance of past victories and miracles? A child might well be upset by missing the celebration of a loved one's birthday even when that loved one had died.

TEXT

Now, if it goes out, does it not require attention? But the following contradicts it: Its observance is from sunset until there is no wayfarer in the street. Does that not mean that if it goes out [within that period], it must be relit? No: if one has not yet lit [it], he must light it; or, in respect of the statutory period: "Until there is no wayfarer in the street." Until when [is that]? Rabba bar Bar Ḥana said in Rabbi Yoḥanan's name: Until the Palmyreans have departed.

INTERPRETATION

A brief halakhic clarification about whether or not one is required to relight a Hanukkah lamp that has gone out provides the first indication that it is required to light the Hanukkah lamp at all. Although this discussion supports the position that the lights do not have to be relit and, therefore, do not require oil and wicks of Sabbath quality, we are finally given to understand, amid all the confusion, that the candles must, at least, be lit. The question now is, why? The gemara approaches this question by first asking, how?

TEXT

Our Rabbis taught: The precept of Hanukkah [demands] one light for each household; the zealous [kindle] a light for each member [of the household]; and the extremely zealous—Beit Shammai maintains: On the first day, eight lights are lit, and thereafter they are gradually reduced; but Beit Hillel says: On the first day one is lit, and thereafter they are progressively increased. Ulla said: In the West [Palestine] two *Amoraim*, Rabbi Yose ben Abin and Rabbi

Yose bar Zabda, differ about this: one maintains: the reason of Beit Shammai is that it shall correspond to the days still to come, and that of Beit Hillel is that it shall correspond to the days that are gone; but the other maintains: Beit Shammai's reason is that it shall correspond to the bullocks of the Festival; while Beit Hillel's reason is that we ascend in [matters of] sanctity, but do not descend.

Rabba bar Bar Hana said in the name of Rabbi Yohanan: There were two old men in Sidon; one followed Beit Shammai, and the other followed Beit Hillel. The former gave as the reason of his action, that it should correspond to the bullocks of the festival, while the latter stated as his reason, because we ascend in [matters of] sanctity but do not descend.

Our Rabbis taught: It is required to place the Hanukkah lamp by the door of one's house on the outside; if one dwells in an upper chamber, he places it at the window nearest the street. But in times of danger it is sufficient to place it on the table. Raba said: Another lamp is required for its light to be used; yet, if there is a blazing fire, it is unnecessary. But in the case of an important person, even if there is a blazing fire, another lamp is required.

INTERPRETATION

The first *tannaitic* source is introduced, describing Hanukkah for the first time as a commandment. That its observance is attested to by Beit Shammai and Beit Hillel, who lived while the Temple stood, is certainly important, yet, it must be pointed out that these *tannaitic* teachings were not included in the codification of the Mishnah. Only in the gemara are they introduced and thereby brought into authoritative rabbinic practice. That Rabbi Judah ha-Nasi saw fit not to include Hanukkah in the mishnah indicates an ambivalence about the festival at a certain stage of rabbinic development—the stage following the destruction of the Temple in Jerusalem.

With this in mind, we learn that there were three opinions concerning how Hanukkah was to be observed. The ordinary person must light one candle per night for his or her household. The zealous person would light one candle per person in the household each night. It is regarding the practice of the extremely zealous that Beit Shammai and Beit Hillel disagree. Beit Shammai teaches that we begin with eight lights on the first day of Hanukkah and that, on each night following, we decrease by one. Beit Hillel teaches that we begin with one light and each night we increase by one. In Palestine, there were two contradictory traditions explaining this dispute. The confusion, by now almost a theme of this passage, continues.

According to one tradition, Beit Shammai reduces the number of lights to correspond to the smaller number of days remaining of the festival, whereas Beit Hillel lights according to the days that are gone. According to the other tradition, Beit Shammai decreases the number of lights to match the decreasing number of sacrificial bullocks brought to the Temple on the eight day festival of Sukkot and Shemini Atzeret, whereas Beit Hillel maintains that the number increases on the basis of a general principle: that we always increase in matters of sanctity, never decrease.

Although no definitive statement choosing between the two traditions is offered, the first is rather simplistic compared with the second. It can be dismissed on the basis of the brief story the gemara now offers. We are told by Rabba bar Bar Ḥana in the name of Rabbi Yoḥanan that there were two old men in Sidon, one of whom followed Beit Shammai and the other, Beit Hillel, and each was able to supply the reason for his master's tradition. The reasons supplied by these Sidonians are the same as the reasons given by Rabbi Yose bar Zabda in our *baraita*. This would seem conclusive.

But just who were these Sidonians, and why is their evidence so telling? Though the gemara does not mention it, the history of Hanukkah is intimately related to the history of Sidon. Sidon is a port town on the coast of Phoenicia, north of the city of Tyre in Lebanon. Long a religious center of the region, Sidon was at various times a wealthy and influential city. First, its natural resources as a port and fishing center established its fame. Later, it was famous as a center for metal craft, carpenters, and lumberers, as well as a center for glassblowing, the technique itself probably having been discovered there. Persia had fully subjugated and largely destroyed the city in the years before the advent of Alexander the Great. Thus, when Alexander, the enemy of Persia, conquered Phoenicia in 333 B.C.E., Sidon surrendered to him gladly and assisted him in the siege of Tyre. Alexander restored Sidon's constitution and territory. In 218 B.C.E., Antiochus III seized Tyre and Ptolemaïs from Ptolemy IV, but Sidon resisted Antiochus and became a center of Ptolemy's operations. But in 200 Antiochus gained Sidon and all of Greek Syria. At the beginning of the Maccabean wars Sidon was a center for staging persecutions of the Jews of Galilee. Simon Maccabee went to the aid of these Jews in 163. In the aftermath of recognition by Pompey in 111, Sidon became an independent city. The edict of Julius Caesar in favor of John Hyrcanus—a Maccabean descendant—and the Jews was set in bronze in Sidon in 47–44 B.C.E. By the first century C.E., large numbers of Jews lived prosperously in Sidon, no doubt carrying with them the legacy of undying loyalty to the Maccabean leadership and of zealous observance of Hanukkah. That the Jews of Sidon could be counted on not only to observe Hanukkah, but to observe it zealously and be aware of the different traditions regarding its observance, must have been still common knowledge in the Amoraic period.

Granting the Sidonian expertise in such matters, what difference was implied between the positions of Beit Shammai and Beit Hillel? Beit Shammai's position is the more straightforward: the observance of Hanukkah is a re-enactment of the rededication of the Temple, itself a re-enactment of the original dedication by Solomon on Sukkot. The lights stand for the sacrifices. Beit Hillel's position is more subtle: the first candle is the one required by law and custom. If we light again the second night, then the principle of "ascending in holiness" applies as well from that night on. Conspicuously absent is any reference to the Temple, and there is certainly no direct correspondence between the lights and the sacrifices. Beit Shammai and Beit Hillel seem to differ on whether Hanukkah takes on holiness in its observance, or, rather, draws its holiness solely from a remembrance of the sacrificial acts of dedication. Thus, even among the zealous observers of Hanukkah, there is disagreement about its nature. What is clear is that, before the destruction of the Temple, Hanukkah was celebrated—had been celebrated for a long time—and that among its celebrants were those whom later tradition would call zealous, though they differed in the reason for their zealousness.

A short *baraita* follows this famous dispute between Beit Shammai and Beit Hillel. It describes the proper placement of the Hanukkah lights—outside the door of the house when possible. We will see below that the placement of the Hanukkah lamp will become an issue of some importance in a larger discussion that points to the holiday's meaning, about which there has still been no firm resolution.

TEXT

What is [the reason for] Hanukkah? For our Rabbis taught: On the twenty-fifth of Kislev [commence] the days of Hanukkah, which

are eight, on which a lamentation for the dead and fasting are forbidden. For when the Greeks entered the Temple, they defiled all
the oils found within it, and when the Hasmonean dynasty prevailed against and defeated them, they made a search and found
only one cruse of oil sealed with the mark of the High Priest, but it
contained sufficient for one day's lighting only; yet a miracle was
wrought and they lit [the lamp] for eight days. The following year
these [days] were appointed a festival with [the recitation of] Hallel and thanksgiving.

INTERPRETATION

At last, the gemara, now confronted with undeniable evidence of the
continuing observance of Hanukkah and still divided as to an appropriate reason for this observance, asks the question we have been asking
all along: "What is [the reason] for Hanukkah?" Again, a *tannaitic*
source is quoted that begins not with the reason but with the practice,
supplies a reason for that practice, and, at the end, expands slightly on
that practice. At no time in this *baraita* is the lighting of a lamp for
Hanukkah mentioned. We are told that on the twenty-fifth of Kislev
begin the eight days of Hanukkah, on which a lamentation for the dead
and fasting are forbidden. The reason for this, we are told, is that the
Greeks had defiled the Temple, and when the Hasmonean dynasty prevailed against them, they searched the Temple for oil with which to
rekindle the Temple Menorah but found only one cruse with the High
Priest's seal of purity, sufficient for only one day's burning. However, a
miracle occurred, and this oil burned for eight days. For this reason, the
following year these eight days were designated as a festival requiring
the recitation of Hallel and thanksgiving.

Only passing reference to the Maccabean victory is made. There is
also no mention of a great rededication ceremony, certainly not one to
rival the dedication ceremony of Solomon on Sukkot, "the festival" of
joy par excellence. Even the miracle of the lights does not yield a festival
of lights. We learn only about the cessation of lamentation for the dead
and fasting.

Recall our question. How do you celebrate the birthday of a loved
one recently deceased? This has now, I suggest, become the question of
our gemara. Hanukkah was, in essence, the rebirth of the Temple. Taken
from the hands of foreigners and returned to the sacred service of Israel, the Temple served as a confirmation of God's abiding care for His

people and more. It served as a confirmation of Israel's merit. If the loss of the Temple could be interpreted as a punishment for Hellenistic assimilation, then its restoration had to be interpreted as a reward for the pious who had withstood that assimilation. From this perspective, Hanukkah represented a rebuke to those living after that same Temple had been destroyed and all attempts at its restoration had failed. That generation was still concerned with lamenting the dead in the wake of the destruction and with fasting to atone for its causes. To them, the joyful observance of Hanukkah had to be problematic, at the very least. However, the popular observance of lighting Hanukkah lamps even into the *amoraic* period must have prompted the Rabbis to lift the veil of lamentation and fasting and also to search for a meaning by which they could justify including Hanukkah in their version of the sacred calendar. That meaning is explored in the following text of the gemara.

TEXT

We learned elsewhere: If a spark that flies from the anvil goes forth and causes damage, he [the smith] is liable. If a camel laden with flax passes through a street, and the flax overflows into a shop, catches fire at the shopkeeper's lamp, and sets the building on fire, the camel owner is liable, but if the shopkeeper placed the light outside, the shopkeeper is liable. Rabbi Judah said: In the case of a Hanukkah lamp he is exempt. Rabina said in Rabba's name: This proves that the Hanukkah lamp should be placed within ten handbreadths. For should you think about ten handbreadths, let him say to him: "you should have placed it higher than a camel and his rider." Yet, perhaps if he is put to too much trouble, he may refrain altogether from the precept.

INTERPRETATION

Having just learned about the reason for observing Hanukkah, and having learned prior to that about the proper placement of the lights, and having learned prior to that about the method for lighting the lamps properly, we now learn a distantly related law concerning civil liability. The mention of the Hanukkah lamp in this *baraita* establishes a connection, but the subject of the *baraita* is liability, not Hanukkah. Are the two related? We will see a profound and complex discussion now between the supporters of Beit Shammai and Beit Hillel. Does Hanukkah mark a celebration derived from the sanctity of the sacrifices of dedication, sacrifices perhaps now symbolically re-enacted by the lighting of lamps? Or does Hanukkah derive its sanctity by virtue of an "ascent in holiness"? Indeed, what constitutes the ascending holiness that the festival encourages?

This *baraita* deals with liability for damages caused by a variety of otherwise permissible activities: the spark that flies from the anvil of a smith, the flax that falls from a camel passing in the street and catches fire at a shopkeeper's lamp. In the first case, the anvil, no conditions are attached. In the second case, the camel owner is liable only if the flax reached into the store to catch fire. If the lamp had been placed outside, the shopkeeper is liable—that is, unless it was a Hanukkah lamp that had been placed outside—proving that the Hanukkah lamp *should* be placed outside. We deduce from this that it should be placed lower than ten handbreadths, for if it could conceivably be placed higher than ten handbreadths, we ought to hold the shopkeeper liable if he did not place the lamp high enough to avoid the camel driver's spilled flax. Yet, the gemara does not unconditionally accept this conclusion, raising the possibility that the Hanukkah lamp need not necessarily be placed below ten handbreadths. The Rabbis did not require the placement of the lamps out of harm's way—perhaps so as to not make observance too burdensome.

A palpable decision has been reached in the text: Hanukkah *is.* Lamentation and fasting for the Temple must cease. But, confronted by the reality of the Temple's destruction, we must enter into the debate between Beit Shammai and Beit Hillel: are the lights a symbolic substitute for the lost sacrifices or for an ascent in holiness beyond the sacrifices? The *baraita* we have been looking at, I suggest, introduces the possibility that our liability—that is, our responsibility—toward our neighbor, has become the new context for understanding the miracle of Hanukkah. Our understanding of God and of our relationship to God (thus far, by the way, never mentioned in our gemara passage) must work itself out in our relationship to our neighbor, not to the Temple. Can this be asking too much? Our passage will conclude by discussing whether the ethics of civil society or ritual re-enactment is the basis for the Hanukkah observance.

TEXT

Rabbi Kahana said Rabbi Nathan ben Minyomi expounded in Rabbi Tanḥum's name that if a Hanukkah lamp is placed above twenty cubits [from the ground] it is unfit, like a *sukkah* and a cross-beam over an alley.

Rabbi Kahana also said, Rabbi Nathan ben Minyomi taught in Rabbi Tanḥum's name: Why is it written, "The pit was empty; there was no water in it" (Gen. 37:24)? From the implication of what is said, "and the pit was empty," do I not know that there was no water in it? What then is taught by, "there was no water in it?" There was no water; yet there were snakes and scorpions in it.

Rabba said: The Hanukkah lamp should be placed within the handbreadth nearest the door. And where is it placed? Rabbi Aḥa son of Raba said: On the right hand side: Rabbi Samuel of Difti said: On the left hand side. And the law is, on the left, so that the Hanukkah lamp shall be on the left and the *mezuzzah* on the right.

INTERPRETATION

The first voice in this discussion is that of Rabbi Tanḥum. He maintains that the Hanukkah lamp may not be placed *higher* than twenty cubits, like the *sukkah* and the crossbeam on a Shabbat *eruv* (the demarcation of a public domain as a private domain through a legal fiction, thus allowing carrying in public on Shabbat). Twenty cubits is much higher than ten handbreadths, yet it is permitted to place the lamp thus, so the shopkeeper is not liable. The ritual of the Hanukkah lamp seems to take precedence over a concern about social ethics! To my mind this reflects the zealousness of the Beit Shammai position that the lighting is but a remembrance of the Temple sacrifices.

A second teaching of Rabbi Tanḥum follows in the text. Its connection with our subject, at first, appears unlikely.

Rabbi Tanḥum introduces the first of the only two biblical verses contained in the entire discussion of Hanukkah in the Talmud. The verse is from the story of Joseph in Genesis and describes the pit into which Joseph's brothers threw him, abandoning him to death. Rabbi Tanḥum points out a seeming superfluity in the verse. Since it says, "The pit was empty" do we not already know that "there was no water in it"? In that case, the phrase, "there was no water in it," must teach us something we would not otherwise know. Rabbi Tanḥum suggests that it teaches us that, although the pit was empty of water, it was not empty of snakes and scorpions. Simple logic might suggest, since this and the previous *baraita* are both taught in Rabbi Tanḥum's name, that they would be consistent with one another and consistent also with Beit Shammai's position, which we have adumbrated. However, the Talmud is not constructed on the canons of simple logic. Rather, the Talmud functions as the world's most finely wrought example of pluralistic logic. In fact, in the face of his earlier teaching, in which Hanukkah can be construed as a reminder of Temple ritual, Rabbi Tanḥum introduces a teaching about social ethics. To be free of direct responsibility for Joseph's death, his brothers place him in an "empty" pit. They appear comforted by the fact that there is no water in it. That makes it safer for Joseph and allows for the possibility of a later return to rescue him. But we find out that, according to Rabbi Tanḥum's interpretation, the opposite was true. Joseph was in even more danger.

We therefore draw the inference that, when Hanukkah was observed as a ritual re-creating the sacrificial observances of the Temple, it lacked an important element. Only by taking seriously the ethical dimension could the Rabbis restore what was lacking. In other words, only if the celebration of Hanukkah combined the views of Beit Shammai and Beit Hillel, could it take its place in the sacred calendar of Judaism.

Raba concludes this section of our text by establishing the halakhah. The Hanukkah lights are to be placed within the handbreadth closest to the door. But on which side? Raba's son says on the right. Rabbi Samuel of Difti says on the left, and the gemara rules that it is the left side, opposite the *mezuzzah*. This appears to reflect the position we have ascribed to Beit Shammai. On the right, the *mezuzzah* reminds us of God's presence and love. On the left, the *ḥanukkiyyah* (Hanukkah menorah) reminds us of the earthly access to this presence and its promise, the Temple.

TEXT

Rabbi Judah said in Rabbi Assi's name: One must not count money by the Hanukkah light. When I stated this before Samuel, he observed to me: "Has the lamp, then sanctity?" Rabbi Joseph demurred: "Does blood possess sanctity? For it was taught: 'he shall pour out its blood and cover it with earth' (Lev. 17:13); when he pours out, he must cover—that is, he must not cover it with his foot, so that precepts may not appear contemptible to him. So here, too, it is that precepts may not appear contemptible to him."

Rabbi Yehoshua ben Levi was asked: "Is it permitted to make use of the *sukkah* decorations during the whole of the seven days?" He answered him [the questioner], "Behold! it was said, One must not count money by the Hanukkah light." "God of Abraham!" exclaimed Rabbi Joseph, "He makes that which was taught dependent upon what was not taught: [of] Sukkot it was taught, whereas of Hanukkah it was not. For it was taught: If one roofs it [the *sukkah*] in accordance with its requirements, beautifies it with hangings and sheets, and suspends in it nuts, peaches, almonds, pomegranates, grape clusters, garlands of ears of corn, wines, oils, and flours; he may not use them until the conclusion of the last day of the feast; yet if he stipulates concerning them, it is all according to his stipulation." Rather, said Rabbi Joseph, the basis of all is [the law relating to] blood.

INTERPRETATION

In an almost theatrical way, the juxtaposition of the Hanukkah lamps and the *mezuzzah* sets the stage for the final section of our text. The gemara will now directly investigate the inherent sanctity of both the Hanukkah lamps and the sacrifices and attempt to resolve the positions of Beit Hillel and Beit Shammai. This process begins with a teaching in Rabbi Assi's name that one may not count money by the Hanukkah light. At first glance this would indicate that the Hanukkah light is sacred, reflecting the position of Beit Shammai. Samuel challenges this position. However, Rabbi Joseph explains that the sanctity of the lights is not an inherent property but rather is analogous to the sanctity of the blood of the sacrifice! For blood, too, does not possess sanctity; yet, when it is poured out, it must be covered with earth. The earth may not be put on it using one's foot, lest the precept appear contemptible—that is to say, both the observance of Hanukkah and the observances connected to the sacrifices can be either valid or not depending upon the attitudes which guide those performing the act. And the ethical stance of the actor is critical to the shaping of those attitudes.

The gemara extends the discussion to include the decorations of the *sukkah*. Our discussion of Hanukkah draws to a close with another reference to Sukkot, the festival of the building of the Tabernacle and the dedication of the Temple. Rabbi Yehoshua ben Levi was asked whether or not it is permissible to use the fruits decorating the *sukkah* for "secular" purposes. He answers by referring to the rule that prohibits counting money by the light of the Hanukkah lamp that we just learned. Rabbi Joseph responds with amazement: How can he make an analogy between Hanukkah and Sukkot when the question about Sukkot has already been answered by a *baraita* that should be the basis for our learning about Hanukkah. Yet, this *baraita* about the Sukkot decorations indicates that they may not normally be used for secular purposes unless a stipulation to this effect is made before Sukkot begins. Such a stipulation ought, then, to be required if one is to count money by the Hanukkah light—an action otherwise forbidden. Thus, we can assume the inherent sanctity of the Hanukkah lights and of the *sukkah* decorations.

Rabbi Joseph seeks to resolve these disputes about the relative holiness of Hanukkah and Sukkot, their relative sanctity and secularity. He also seeks to resolve the dispute about the relative importance of ritual versus ethical considerations, thereby also resolving the dispute between Beit Shammai and Beit Hillel. He accomplishes all of this with one phrase: "The basis of all is the blood." Our final task is to unpack this phrase.

The seventeenth chapter of Leviticus is concerned almost entirely with the prohibition against eating blood. It begins by asserting that anyone attempting to sacrifice an animal must do so at the single proper altar at the door of the Tent of Meeting. It then describes the proper way of disposing of the blood of the animal and adds the prohibition against consuming any blood. It teaches that animals and fowl for private consumption must also be drained of blood, which is then covered with earth. Finally, the chapter ends with a prohibition of eating flesh from carcasses of dead animals or flesh torn from a living beast. The blood of the sacrifice is, however, used on the altar as the central instrument of expiation. The rationale for the use and disposition of the blood is not only stated but repeated: "For the life of all flesh—its blood is its life. . . . for the life of all flesh is its blood" (Lev. 17:14).

Rabbi Joseph has managed a transformation of major proportions. Blood is the agent of expiation. The destruction of the Temple was viewed as having occurred as a result of sin. The sin of *sinat ḥinam*, "baseless hatred" among the people of Israel, is one often cited. How is sin to be expiated in the absence of the Temple? "The basis of all is the blood." The Hanukkah lights, a remembrance of the sacrifices according to Beit Shammai, can function as a symbol of the blood; this is an expiatory function. But the expiation of sin cannot be accomplished without our developing a sense of responsibility for one another. Granted that without a symbolic re-enactment of the Temple's presence, expiation for sin is impossible, but it is equally impossible without changing how we relate to one another. The holiness we must attain in a world blighted by the destruction of the Temple must ascend beyond symbolic expiation. It must change the ways in which we behave toward one another. About such behavior we must indeed be among the "most zealous."

On the birthday of those who are not long dead we cease our mourning, our fasting and lamentation. We remember their birth with joy for the life it gave them and which we shared, and we attempt in our own lives to embody the best values for which they stood. Those values account for the persistence of the Hanukkah celebration and the reason the Rabbis accepted it and imbued it with new meaning.

The author wishes to acknowledge the assistance and joy provided by Daniel Huberman, who learned this gemara with him in preparation for his Bar Mitzvah.

YOU MUST BE CRAZY
TO SPEAK OF REDEMPTION
Purim and a Conclusion of Sorts

Megillah 3a–3b

TEXT

Now that you have decided that the words "city and city" have a homiletical purpose, what is the purpose of the words "family and family" [in the same verse] (Esth. 9:28)? Rabbi Yose ben Ḥanina replied: This contains a reference to the families of the priests and Levites, that they should desist from their service in order to come and hear the reading of the megillah. For so said Rabbi Judah in the name of Rav: The priests at their service, the Levites on their platform, the lay Israelites at their stations—all desist from their service in order to hear the reading of the megillah. It has been taught to the same effect: priests at their service, Levites on their platforms, lay Israelites at their station—all desist from their service in order to come and hear the reading of the megillah. It was in reliance on this dictum that the members of the house of Rabbi were wont to desist from the study of Torah in order to come and hear the reading of the megillah. They argued *a fortiori* from the case of the service. If the service, which is so important, may be abandoned, how much more the study of the Torah?

INTERPRETATION

It is often the case that jokes, jests, slips of the tongue, visions, and dreams all contribute to expressing a person's true feelings. Anyone who has celebrated Purim and heard the reading of the scroll of Esther amid the riotousness permitted and encouraged in the synagogue at that time should not be surprised at this fact. It may be essential for people to "let down their hair" now and then in order to express their most cherished values, for under the pressure of our otherwise very serious day to day lives, these values can become obscured or even purposely hidden.

The Book of Esther is a very human book, a purposely comic book, in which the name of God does not appear. Everything that happens, happens by accident. Secrets are revealed inadvertently, plots are hatched and uncovered, and the bad guys suffer what they'd planned for the good guys. Yet, the seriousness with which the Book of Esther is approached by the gemara and the seriousness of the obligation to hear the book read aloud suggest the tradition's understanding that the search for truth must be redoubled amid the levity. It may also suggest that the search for certain truths can occur *only* amid the levity. Tractate *Megillah* is, therefore, not humorous. Rather, it uses the occasion of all this humor to reassess the most cherished ideals of the rabbinic enterprise.

We join the gemara in the midst of a discussion of the purpose of some rather obvious repetition in the Book of Esther. The hermeneutical principle guiding this discussion posits that the Tanakh (Hebrew Scriptures), being of divine authorship, does not contain a single unnecessary word. Therefore, a repeated word, a word not absolutely necessary to carry the narrative, must have been intended to convey some additional information. In our case, the entire verse under discussion reads:

Consequently, these days are recalled and observed in every generation [*dor va-dor*]: by every family [*mishpakhah u-mishpakhah*] every province [*medinah u-medinah*). And every city [*ir va-ir*] and these days of Purim shall never cease among the Jews, and the memory of them shall never perish among their descendants. (Esth. 9:28)

The focus of our passage, as the first line announces, is to deduce the purpose of the repetition of the word "family." Rabbi Yose ben Ḥanina suggests the purpose: to teach us that the families of the priests and the Levites should desist from their Temple service in order to hear the reading of the megillah. His position is supported by two *beraitot,* one in the name of Rav and one in the name of an anonymous *Tanna* (teacher from the period of the Mishnah) on the basis of which the members of the house of Rabbi Judah ha-Nasi (head of the assembly, also known simply as "Rabbi"), the compiler of the Mishnah and among its most authoritative teachers, would desist from the study of Torah in order to hear the megillah read. They deduced the appropriateness of this practice by an *a fortiori* argument—that is, if the Temple service, which is so important, is interrupted in order to hear the megillah read, how much more is Torah study, which is less important than the Temple service, also to be interrupted. It is this last assertion that occasions a full investigation of the relative importance of these various activities: Temple service, Torah study, hearing the megillah read, involvement with other rituals, and, finally, concern for the dignity of other people.

TEXT

But *is* the service more important than the study of the Torah? Surely it is written: "Once, when Joshua was near Jericho, he looked up and saw a man standing before him, . . . Joshua threw himself face down to the ground"(Josh. 5:13). Now how could he do such a thing, seeing that Rabbi Yehoshua ben Levi has said that it is forbidden for a man to greet another by night, for fear that he may be a demon? It was different there, because he said to him 'I am captain of the LORD's host' (Josh. 5:14). But perhaps he was lying? We take it for granted that they do not utter the name of heaven vainly. He said to him: "This evening you neglected the regular afternoon sacrifice, and now you have neglected the study of Torah." Joshua replied: "In regard to which of them have you come?" He answered, "Now I have come" (Josh. 5:14). "This was after Joshua had spent the night in the valley *[ha-emek]*" (Josh. 8:13), and Rabbi Yoḥanan said: This shows that he tarried in the depths *[umkah]* of the halakhah. And Rabbi Samuel ben Unia also said: The study of the Torah is greater than the offering of the daily sacrifices, as it says, "Now I have come." There is no contradiction; in the one case [the study] of an individual is meant; in the other, that of the whole people.

But is that of an individual unimportant? Have we not learned: Women [when mourning] on a festival make a dirge, but do not beat the breast. Rabbi Ishmael says: If they are near the bier, they can beat the breast. On the New Moon, Hanukkah, and Purim they may make a dirge and beat the breast, but on neither the one nor the other do they wail; and in reference to this, Rabba ben Ḥuna said: A major festival involves no restrictions in the case of a scholar, still less Hanukkah and Purim. You are speaking of the honor to be paid to the Torah. The honor to be paid to the learning of an individual is important, whereas the study of an individual is [comparatively] unimportant.

INTERPRETATION

The gemara begins with a challenge to the assertion that Temple service is more important than Torah study. However, in the course of this challenge, and before we can actually assess its place in the argument, we must unravel a complex and seemingly unrelated digression upon which this challenge is based.

The assertion that Torah study is more important than Temple service is based on an exegesis of two verses in the chapter 5 of the Book of Joshua and one verse in the chapter 8 of the same book. The first verse occurs after Joshua has led the people of Israel into the Promised Land across the Jordan, after the mass circumcision of all the Jewish men born in the wilderness, the first observance of Pesaḥ in the new land, and before the great battle of Jericho. The second occurs in the night between the preparations for war and the beginning of the battle at Ai.

At Jericho, Joshua is alone at night. He has completed an ambitious program of spiritual renewal among the people. He has reinstated the covenant of circumcision and the Paschal sacrifice. He has thus set the religious tone of the coming struggle for the land. Alone and presumably reflective, he meets a man—a stranger who has appeared out of nowhere. In answer to Joshua's query, "Are you one of us or one of our enemies?" Joshua hears the stranger say, "No, I am captain of the LORD's host. Now I have come!" Joshua falls on his face in prostration. Joshua asks what this messenger of God commands. He is told only to remove his sandals because the ground he is on is holy. With this, chapter 5 concludes. Chapter 6 follows, with the miraculous destruction of the walls of Jericho.

The gemara restructures this story of the meeting between Joshua and the captain of the Lord's host by following it with a verse from chapter 8 of the Book of Joshua. We read, "This was after Joshua had spent the night in the valley" (Josh. 8:13). The gemara constructs a conversation between Joshua and his interlocutor that is missing from the biblical text. Before constructing this conversation by freely using unconnected verses, the gemara interrupts itself and questions how Joshua could have spoken to the stranger he met in the night in the first place. He would have been forbidden to do so halakhically! Rabbi Yehoshua ben Levi taught that it is forbidden for a person to greet another at night, for fear that the stranger might be a demon. But in our case, since the messenger identified himself as the captain of the Lord's host, the situation is different. Joshua knew that the man was not a demon. But the question is raised: perhaps the stranger was lying? The answer to this question is: We have a tradition that even demons do not utter the name of God in vain. Therefore, this "being" who identified himself by God's name could not have lied.

This digression is a rich vein of foreshadowing. The story in which Torah study, here symbolized by halakhah, is put forward as more important than Temple worship contains a critique of Joshua for having violated halakhah. The gemara answers this critique by responding that Joshua did not violate halakhah; rather he reached beyond the law to allow a stranger to identify himself by the name of God. Remember that Rabbi Yehoshua ben Levi teaches that it is forbidden to greet a man by night. But had Joshua not sent forth his greeting, the stranger would not have been able to identify himself. Only by seeming to violate the law could Joshua be vindicated by an exception to the law. This digression cuts to the heart of what is at stake in this entire passage: We learn the godly status of strangers when we break the safety of the silence between us and them.

The gemara, of course, does not explicitly reach this conclusion. Rather, it changes the order of the conversation between the stranger and Joshua so that the stranger speaks first! Joshua is saved from violating the halakhah of Rabbi Yehoshua ben Levi. Instead, he is accused of violating the halakhah concerning the importance of sacrifice versus study. Joshua has neglected them both, but the Lord's messenger teaches him what he did wrong. In a sense, Joshua is rescued from his violation because he is engaging in Torah study with the stranger. The stranger points out that Joshua has neglected that day's afternoon sacrifice and that evening's Torah study. On the basis of which of these transgressions did the Lord feel Joshua deserved to be rebuked? The messenger answers, "Now I have come"—that is, I have come regarding Torah study. Immediately the gemara invokes the verse from chapter 8, that Joshua tarried in the midst of the valley by night, indicating that he immediately undertook to study Torah. Finally, we learn from Rabbi Samuel ben Unia that Rabbi Yoḥanan's interpretation of the verse in chapter 8 could equally have been derived simply from the verse in chapter 5: "Now I have come."

The Talmud's extended exegesis of these verses in the Book of Joshua leaves us with a contradiction. If this exegesis is correct, then Torah study is more important than Temple service. If this is the case, then the household of Rabbi Judah ha-Nasi made an invalid inference—abandoning the Temple service to hear the reading of the megillah should not be taken as a reason to abandon Torah study in order to hear the megillah read. The gemara resolves this contradiction by asserting that the law derived from the verses in Joshua refers to communal Torah study, which takes precedence over the Temple service, while the case derived from the example of Rabbi Judah ha-Nasi refers to individual Torah study, which is less important than performing the Temple service.

The gemara briefly takes up the question of whether or not such a distinction between personal Torah study and communal Torah study is legitimate. In doing so it raises two important subjects: first, the value of respect for human beings, and, second, the relationship between communal and individual values. Both subjects are raised through reference to a *baraita* that restricts the honor to be paid the dead on major festivals and minor festivals such as Hanukkah or Purim. These restrictions are not, according to Rabba ben Ḥuna, applicable to Torah scholars. This would seem to indicate that the honor due to a Torah scholar is in no way reduced by the community's celebration of festivals and, therefore, challenges the distinction we've made that communal study and ritual practice are of greater value than individual study and practice. However, the gemara goes on to distinguish between the honor due a Torah scholar who dies and the act of a scholar studying Torah who becomes a mourner. The latter is, in fact, restricted and subjected to the community's norms.

We now have all the elements of the larger question of our passage: Which takes precedence among three competing claims: Temple service, Torah study (as a community), or the respect for human beings exemplified by the laws of mourning.

TEXT

Raba said: There is no question in my mind that, as between the Temple service and the reading of the megillah, the reading of the megillah takes priority, for the reason given by Rabbi Yose ben Ḥanina. As between the study of the Torah and the reading of the megillah, the reading of the megillah takes priority, since the members of the house of Rabbi based themselves [on the teaching of Rabbi Yose]. As between the study of Torah and attending to a *meit mitzvah* (a deceased person with no one else to tend to its burial), attending to a *meit mitzvah* takes precedence, since it has been taught: The study of the Torah may be neglected in order to perform the last rites or to bring a bride to the canopy. As between the Temple service and attending to a *meit mitzvah*, attending to a *meit mitzvah* takes precedence, as we learn from the text, "or sister" (Num. 6:7), as it has been taught: "Or sister": what is the point of these words? Suppose he was on his way to kill his Paschal lamb or to circumcise his son, and he heard that a near relative had died, shall I assume that he should defile himself? You must say, he should not defile himself. Shall I assume then that, just as he does not defile himself for his sister, so he should not defile himself for a *meit mitzvah?* It says significantly, "or sister"; it is for his sister that he may not defile himself, but he may defile himself for a *meit mitzvah.* Raba propounded the questions: as between reading of the megillah and [attending to] a *meit mitzvah,* which takes precedence? Shall I say that the reading of the megillah takes precedence in order to proclaim the miracle, or does, perhaps, [the burying of] the *meit mitzvah* take precedence because of the respect due to human beings? After propounding the question, he himself answered it saying, [burying] the *meit mitzvah* takes precedence since a master has said: Great is the [obligation to pay due] respect to human beings, since it overrides a negative precept of the Torah.

INTERPRETATION

Raba expounds, without contradiction, that the reading of the megillah takes precedence over the Temple service. He bases himself on Rabbi Yose ben Ḥanina's exegesis of the repeated word "family," with which our passage began. Raba also admits the deduction that Rabbi Judah ha-Nasi's school made from Rabbi Yose's exegesis—that is, that Torah study, too, is interrupted for the reading of the megillah. He then proceeds to explain why respect for human beings takes precedence over Temple, Torah, and megillah.

Beginning with a comparison between the study of Torah and attending to a *meit mitzvah*, a deceased person with no one else to tend to its burial, attending a *meit mitzvah* takes precedence. This is taught on the basis of a *baraita*: "The study of Torah may be neglected in order to perform the last rites or to bring a bride to the canopy."

Regarding the comparison between Temple service and attending a *meit mitzvah*, attending the *meit mitzvah* also takes precedence, according to that which is learned from the exegesis of the phrase "or sister" in the Book of Numbers (6:7), the law of the Nazirite. Again, the basis of the exegesis is a perceived redundancy in the text. The Torah teaches that a *nazir* (a person who enters a temporary state of priestly service), like the High Priest, should not defile himself by proximity to the dead, even if the deceased is his father, mother, brother, or his sister. The Talmud, in Tractate *Nazir*, considers the phrase "or sister" to be superficially redundant. It asks: Couldn't we have deduced the inclusion of his sister from the other relationships mentioned? Why does the Torah include this phrase? Rabbinic assumption holds that the Torah does not supply information that could have been easily deduced by the application of reason. The discussion in Tractate *Nazir* concludes that the inclusion of this seemingly superfluous phrase is intended to teach that even if a Nazirite is on his way to perform the Paschal sacrifice, or to circumcise his son, obligations the neglect of which are punishable by *koret*, being "cut off" from Israel, he is required to defile himself immediately and to attend to the needs of the *meit mitzvah*.

Finally, Raba asks and answers the question: Which takes precedence: the reading of the megillah or attending a *meit mitzvah*? We might have thought that the importance of publicizing the miracle of Purim took precedence. Raba teaches that it does not. He quotes a general principle of rabbinic teaching: "Great is the obligation to pay due respect to human beings, since it overrides a negative precept of the Torah."

Sections of the Talmud that seem to speak in a single, authoritative voice are far less common than sections that are loud with differing voices. The univocal quality of this final selection cannot be considered either unintended or unimportant. The creation of a pluralistic discourse that is the Talmud's main aim appears to have failed us here. There appears to be agreement.

If we assume that the world is always on the brink of violence, then a pluralistic discourse able to counter the onset of this violence must be never-ending. In that case, redemption, the cessation of the threat of violence, is not possible. And without redemption, without the possibility of redemption, meaning itself is always tentative, always relative, and at worst, impossible. If, on the other hand, we posit, as Jewish tradition does, the possibility of meaning, if history is the journey toward redemption, then at some moment it is necessary that pluralistic discourse give way to a postulate—what we might see as a redemptive postulate. What better time and place for this to occur than amid the laughter of Purim! Only when our mouths are filled with laughter, when the evil ones have been hanged on their own gallows, when we've drunk a little too much whiskey, can we dare to imagine a world whose meaning is fulfilled, a world whose meaning is itself. Amid the levity of Purim we can say those things that otherwise would appear to be crazy: the Temple service can be put aside, the Torah can be neglected, the reading of the megillah can be viewed as unimportant. What is important—and the essence of redemption—is that we treat our fellow human beings with supreme respect. God's name is missing from the megillah because it isn't needed; the face of a human being is there instead.

It is no accident that this level of respect for the face of a person can be conveyed best in the example of a corpse. Our intuition of redemption always comes too late; it is often present only in confrontation with death. The death of another is a commanding reminder of our failure to have prevented that death, even as it is an intimation of our limitations in the face of death. The rabbinic idea of the resurrection of the dead reminds us of what *we* cannot do and of what is ultimately at stake in redemption.

Thus, the give and take of discourse breaks off for a moment. The redemptive possibility of a time when peace itself no longer requires an endless discourse is introduced. It is a bit of a joke, the slip of a tongue that has tasted a drop too much. It passes, and the sea of Talmud closes seamlessly around it and goes on.

SELECTED BIBLIOGRAPHY

WORKS BY EMMANUEL LEVINAS AVAILABLE IN ENGLISH

Bold initials indicate references in the text.

BTV *Beyond the Verse.* Translated by Gary D. Mole. Bloomington: Indiana University Press, 1994.

CPP *Collected Philosophical Papers.* Translated by Alphonso Lingis. The Hague: Martinus Nijhoff, 1987.

EE *Existence and Existents.* Translated by Alphonso Lingis. The Hague: Martinus Nijhoff, 1978.

EI *Ethics and Infinity.* Translated by Richard A. Cohen. Pittsburgh: Duquesne University Press, 1985.

NTR *Nine Talmudic Readings.* Translated by Annette Aronowicz. Bloomington: Indiana University Press, 1990.

OBBE *Otherwise Than Being or Beyond Essence.* Translated by Alphonso Lingis. Dordrecht: Kluwer Academic Publishers, 1991.

OTS *Outside the Subject.* Translated by Michael B. Smith. Stanford: Stanford University Press, 1994.

THI *The Theory of Intuition in Husserl's Phenomenology.* Translated by André Orianne. Evanston: Northwestern University Press, 1973.

TI *Totality and Infinity.* Translated by Alphonso Lingis. Pittsburgh: Duquesne University Press, 1969.

TO *Time and the Other.* Translated by Richard A. Cohen. Pittsburgh: Duquesne University Press, 1987.

TON *In the Time of Nations.* Translated by Michael B. Smith. Bloomington: Indiana University Press, 1994.

STUDIES OF EMMANUEL LEVINAS

Bernasconi, Robert and David Wood, ed. *The Provocation of Levinas.* London: Routledge, 1988.

Bernasconi, Robert and Simon Critchley, ed. *Re-Reading Levinas.* Bloomington: Indiana University Press, 1991.

Cohen, Richard, ed. *Face to Face with Levinas.* Albany, NY: State University of New York Press, 1986.

ELEV Cohen, Richard. *Elevations.* Chicago: University of Chicago Press, 1994.

CRL Gibbs, Robert. *Correlations in Rosenzweig and Levinas.* Princeton, NJ: Princeton University Press, 1992.

Hand, Sean, ed. *The Levinas Reader.* Oxford: Basil Blackwell, 1989.

FOR Handelman, Susan. *Fragments of Redemption.* Bloomington: Indiana University Press, 1991.

Llewelyn, John. *The Genealogy of Ethics: Emmanuel Levinas.* London: Routledge, 1995.

Manning, Robert John Sheffler. *Interpreting Otherwise Than Heidegger.* Pittsburgh: Duquesne University Press, 1993.

Ouaknin, Marc-Alain. *The Burnt Book.* Translated by Llewelyn Brown. Princeton, NJ.: University of Princeton Press, 1995.

Valevicius, Andrius. *From the Other to the Totally Other.* New York: Peter Lang, 1988.

Wyschogrod, Edith. *Emmanuel Levinas: The Problem of Ethical Metaphysics.* The Hague: Martinus Nijhoff, 1974.

INDEX OF BIBLICAL PASSAGES

INDEX